PUB WALKS

The Midshires way

TWENTY CIRCULAR WALKS IN
LEICESTERSHIRE, NOTTINGHAMSHIRE
AND DERBYSHIRE

Peter Fooks

COUNTRYSIDE BOOKS
NEWBURY, BERKSHIRE

COUNTRYSIDE BOOKS
3 Catherine Road
Newbury, Berkshire

ISBN 1 85306 398 3

Designed by Mon Mohan
Cover illustration by Colin Doggett
Photographs by the author
Maps by S. R. Lyons

Produced through MRM Associates Ltd., Reading
Typeset by The Midlands Book Typesetting Company, Loughborough
Printed and bound by J.W. Arrowsmith Ltd., Bristol

Contents

Publisher's Note

We hope that you obtain considerable enjoyment from this book; great care has been taken in its preparation. However, changes of landlord and actual closures are sadly not uncommon. Likewise, although at the time of publication all routes followed public rights of way or permitted paths, diversion orders can be made and permissions withdrawn.

We cannot of course be held responsible for such diversion orders and any inaccuracies in the text which result from these or any other changes to the routes nor any damage which might result from walkers trespassing on private property. However, we are anxious that all details covering the walks and the pubs are kept up to date and would therefore welcome information from readers which would be relevant to future editions.

Introduction

This book *Pub Walks along the Midshires Way* deals with the northern half of the trail – the 136 miles (approximately) from the river Welland, on the Northamptonshire border, through Leicestershire, Nottinghamshire and Derbyshire to the Metropolitan Borough of Stockport.

The Midshires Way is a far less demanding route than many other long-distance paths. It has a special charm of its own and will appeal to walkers of all levels of experience. A particular quality is that, while the route tends to avoid the popular beauty spots, such as Charnwood Forest and Dovedale, it threads its way through some of the most charming and unsung areas of the English Midlands – the rolling wolds of Leicestershire with their thatched cottages and golden churches, the red brick and pantile villages of South Nottinghamshire, the grit and limestone hills and dales of Derbyshire. And in the course of that journey it follows a multitude of traditional paths and tracks through a fascinating and varied landscape moulded by many generations.

The Midshires Way is essentially a multi-user recreational route – that is to say, it is intended for use by walkers, cyclists and equestrians. This being a book of pub walks, where there is a choice of route, it will, of course, be the pedestrian alternative that we offer. Through Leicestershire, the Way is the same for all users, which means that the full distance through the county follows roads, tracks and bridleways accessible to horses. The route is generally easy to follow, and much of the waymarking, particularly over the larger 'prairies' is supplemented with tall, yellow-painted posts – a tremendous help.

The Nottinghamshire section offers alternatives over much of the Way. In the nature of things, footpaths tend to be rather more adventurous than bridlepaths – more stiles to climb, for instance – but they also tend to be quieter, and more intimate.

Walkers are well provided for in Derbyshire, and here it is the horse-riders who at present lack full provision. There is a splendid variety of footpaths, bridleways, green lanes, abandoned railways and canal towpaths to ring the changes, and the waymarking, whether by guide-posts, arrow-discs, or double-acorn Midshires Way logos, is generally excellent.

Apart from the routes themselves, the scenery offers plenty of variety. Throughout Leicestershire and Nottinghamshire, and into south Derbyshire, the countryside reflects the typical arable/livestock agricultural pattern of the region, with a mixture of large arable and smaller grass fields, interspersed with stands of broadleaved woodland.

The Midshires Way here does not follow any other officially designated routes, although it does cross the Leicestershire Round from time to time, and it is clear from the nature of many of the tracks – ridgeways, hollow ways, and paths aligned on church spires – that most are very ancient.

Quite early in the journey north, the first reminder is encountered that the character of these north Midlands counties has been largely shaped by the industry of man. The mighty power station at Ratcliffe on Soar dominates for much of the way, and is in view for at least 40 miles of the route. A variety of arteries are met on the 'three-counties boundary' near Shardlow, with the M1 motorway, the A6 trunk road, the Trent and Mersey Canal and the rivers Trent and Derwent all vying for attention.

As the route proceeds northward into Derbyshire, it skirts the semi-industrial areas between Nottingham and Derby, before heading onward into the beauties of the Peak District. Again, this is an area very much shaped by man over many centuries – the lead miners of central Derbyshire, for example, and the industrialists of the Derwent valley. The Way follows, for a while, possibly the oldest road in Derbyshire, the Old Portway. But for many more miles it follows the traditionally interrelated routes of the High Peak Railway and the Peak Forest Canal.

Between Whaley Bridge and Compstall, the route follows the Goyt Way, alternating between the river Goyt and the Peak Forest Canal. Then, from here to the end of the line in Stockport, the Valley Way takes over, still following, fairly faithfully, the river Goyt.

It is quite likely that some of our readers will be proposing to follow the Midshires Way in full. For that reason, we have provided basic details, at the end of each chapter, of the various stages of the route. But these are not intended to be comprehensive, and you are recommended to obtain the official Midshires Way Pack and the appropriate Ordnance Survey maps.

Our real object is to provide a series of short circular walks along the Way, all within the capacity of the average casual walker, and all incorporating a good family pub, where the food, the drink and the company are of the best. Each walk includes a section of the Midshires Way, and has been selected to provide, as far as possible, an easy and attractive ramble for the entire family. The walking distance has been kept as reasonable as conditions permit, the longest walk being 5³/₄ miles and the shortest alternative route 2¹/₄. Perhaps, when you have completed all the walks, you will be inspired to fill in the gaps! We can certainly recommend it.

As with the southern Midshires Way book, this one has been a joint effort. My wife has assisted me in the surveying of most of the routes –

and has called me to order when I looked like getting lost! The Leisure Services departments of Leicestershire, Nottinghamshire and Derbyshire have all been of help in verifying the existence of rights of way. And, in the interests of consistency, the sketch maps, although based on my own first drafts, have been prepared in more professional form by Sally Lyons.

Good Walking!

Peter Fooks
Spring 1996

Key for Maps

●●●●●●●● Midshires Way

⑬ Location of Pub Walk

→ → Pub Walk

●●●→●●● Pub Walk incorporating Midshires Way

Midshires Way – overall route from the Ridgeway to the Pennines.

Midshires Way – Northamptonshire border to Hoby, Leicestershire. (25 miles)

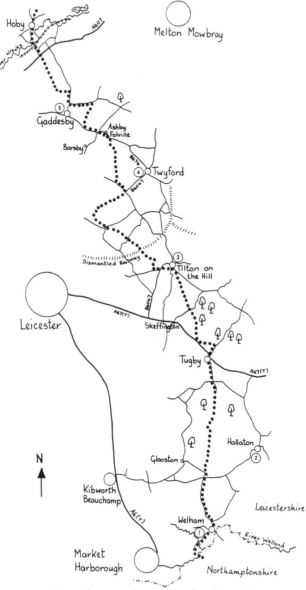

Map showing location of Pub Walks 1–5.

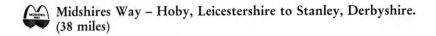

Midshires Way – Hoby, Leicestershire to Stanley, Derbyshire. (38 miles)

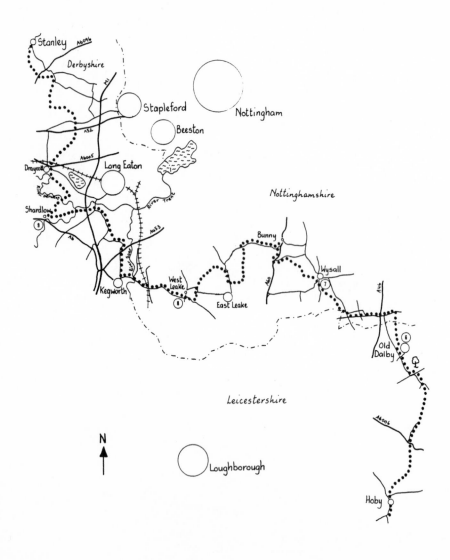

Map showing location of Pub Walks 6–9.

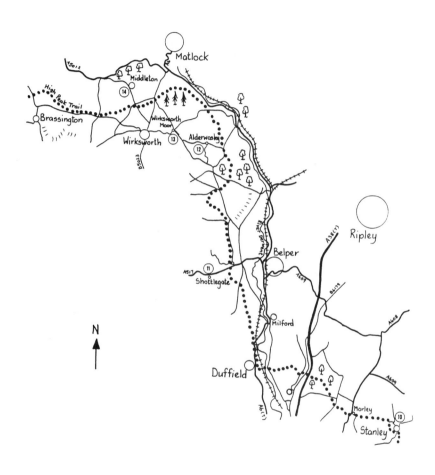

Map showing location of Pub Walks 10–14.

Midshires Way – Longcliffe to Buxton. (21 miles)

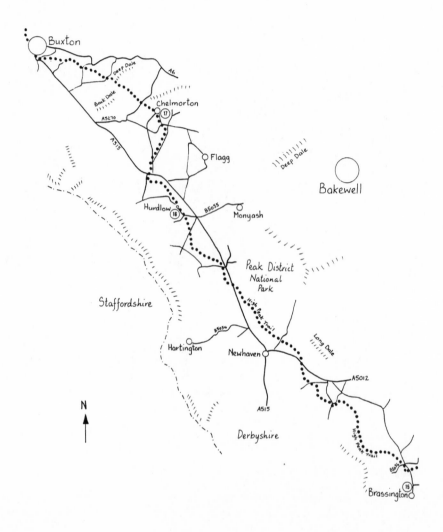

Map showing location of Pub Walks 15–17.

Midshires Way – Buxton, Derbyshire to Stockport, Gt. Manchester. (28 miles)

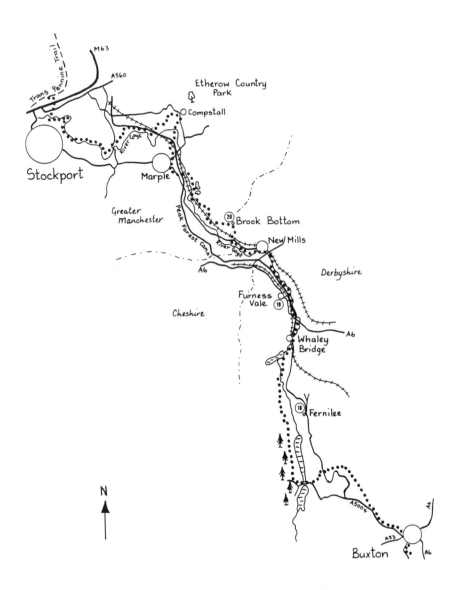

Map showing location of Pub Walks 18–20.

[1]   Welham
The Old Red Lion

The tiny village of Welham lies at a junction of five quiet lanes, right on the edge of Leicestershire, and its seclusion is so absolute that the popularity of its inn comes as a complete surprise. The Old Red Lion is a busy and attractive freehouse, which has been tastefully modernised.

Food is available daily and evenings, orders being accepted until half an hour before closing. The management stipulate that this is a pub, not a restaurant – a fact reflected in the reasonable prices. You can choose from a comprehensive range of steaks, seafood and snacks. The *pièce de résistance* is the Zeppelin – a massive 48 ounce rump steak, definitely better after the walk than before! We can, however, recommend the delicious steak and kidney or chicken and mushroom pies, or the filled jacket potatoes or ploughman's lunch. Families are welcome here and there is a special children's menu, as well as vegetarian dishes. The selection of ales includes both Tetley Bitter and Pedigree, lagers on offer are XXXX, Carlsberg and Lowenbrau, and Olde English cider is also available on draught.

Weekday opening hours are from 11.30 am to 2.30 pm and 6 pm to 11 pm. Sunday has all-day opening, from noon until 10.30 pm.

Telephone: 01858 565253.

How to get there: From the A6 Leicester to Market Harborough road, turn off at the B6047 (Melton Mowbray) turning, travelling north. Turn east as you approach Church Langton, passing through Thorpe Langton and continuing straight on to Welham. The Old Red Lion is past the church, on the left.

Parking: Patrons may leave their vehicles in the pub car park while they walk – but ask first, particularly if you have a large party with several cars.

Length of the walk: 5 miles. Maps: OS Landranger 141 Kettering and Corby, and Pathfinder 916 Wigston and Kibworth Beauchamp (inn GR 767926).

This truly delightful walk commences with a steady, but gentle ascent of Burrow Hill. There are few stiles, and those there are can be easily negotiated. And the views over the surrounding country provide both a fitting farewell to Northamptonshire and a splendid introduction to Leicestershire.

The Walk

Turn right and follow the road past the church, round the right-hand bend and on. At the next, leftward, bend, leave the road, following the waymarked bridleway straight ahead. Continue, with the hedge on your right until it bends away to the right, then bear left to reach a gate in the far top corner of the field.

Pass through the gate and continue ahead, now on the left of the hedge, following the overhead lines. Keep to the hedgeside over three fields, passing a long-abandoned pit in the second, now grassed over and fitting into the contours of the field. Sometimes partly flooded, it adds an idyllic extra touch to the walk.

At the end of the third field, pass through the gateway. The Pathfinder map shows the path as following a direct line over the next three fields to reach the summit of Burrow Hill, but popular usage, with a crop in the ground, clearly favours the hedgeside – follow the hedge round the end of the field to reach a gate in the opposite hedge, near the top of the rise. Pass through the gate and continue, again on the left of the hedge, and past a new plantation. Turn left at the top of the field and continue to a handgate. Pass through and on, to the edge of the field, turning right again and continuing to the summit trig point.

The summit (147 metres or 482 ft) is a good place to pause for a few minutes. There are several large stones available and the views are fine in every direction. Just to the right of your route of ascent, directly behind a handgate, you can see the spire of Thorpe Langton church.

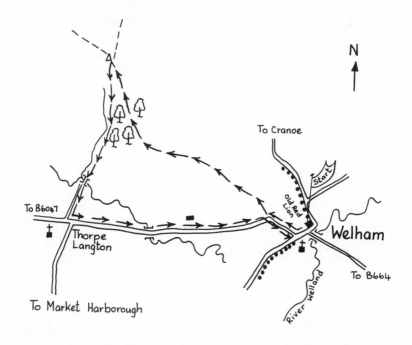

Retrace your steps along the left of the hedge to reach and cross a stile. Keep straight forward over the next field, passing through Fox Covert, and bearing right to reach a stile beside a farm gate. Continue, making directly towards Thorpe Langton, with a farm lane clearly in view ahead. Cross a stile and a footbridge to reach the lane, and follow this to Thorpe Langton.

Turn left at the road and continue along it to return to Welham. The Midshires Way is joined on the bend by the church, where a track joins the village street from the right.

Midshires Way – river Welland, south of Welham, to Cranoe (4 miles)

The Way crosses the river, the Northamptonshire/Leicestershire border, on a gated wooden bridge, continuing over the field to Welham Road, where it turns right. This is a metalled road, but the wayfarer is unlikely to meet any vehicular traffic, because the bridge over an intervening stream is too narrow for anything broader than a horse. At Welham the lane joins the village street, passing the Old Red Lion and turning left, taking the left fork at the next junction and continuing along this quiet road to the Tur Langton to Hallaton road and the little village of Cranoe.

[2]   Hallaton
The Fox Inn

The south Leicestershire village of Hallaton is, without doubt, one of the most picturesque in the county, with its cheerful blend of red brick, golden stone and traditional thatch, and its striking Butter Cross. A time-honoured 'bottle-kicking' event takes place here, every year on Easter Monday, the bottle being a small wooden cask of ale. The contest takes place at Hare Pie Hill, where a hare pie is thrown to the crowd, following a procession from the Fox Inn.

The inn itself occupies a charming situation on the very edge of the village, beside the attractive duck pond. An ancient building, its interior is full of old-world charm. Particularly eye catching are a number of seats adapted from empty barrels, and the impressive bare-brick wall which surrounds the open fireplace. Food is available every lunchtime and evening from Tuesday to Sunday. Monday is the cook's day off – except on bank holidays. A full and varied menu offers a wide selection of flesh, fish and fowl, all served with either fresh vegetables or salad. The regular bar meals include jumbo sausages, chicken and leek pie, ploughman's platter and steak and mushroom pie. There is a separate vegetarian menu, and a selection of delicious sandwiches. Families are welcome at the Fox, and will also enjoy the excellent picnic and play area close to the duck pond. Well-behaved dogs are allowed, but only in the garden area.

The brewery is Ansells, and ales on offer include both Tetley Bitter and Marston's Pedigree. If lager is your choice there is Castlemaine and Carlsberg Export, alongside Olde English for the cider drinker. There is an extensive wine list.

The opening hours are from 11 am to 3 pm and 7 pm to 11 pm on Monday to Saturday. Sunday opening is from 12 noon to 3 pm and 7 pm to 10.30 pm.

Telephone: 01858 555278.

How to get there: From the A47 Leicester to Peterborough trunk road, turn south through Tugby village, following the Hallaton road signs. The Fox Inn will be seen on the left, beside the pond, as you enter the village.

Parking: You are welcome to leave your car in the extensive pub car park while you take your walk. Some on-street parking is also available in the village.

Length of the walk: 5³/₄ miles. Maps: OS Landranger 141 Kettering and Corby, and Pathfinder 916 Wigston and Kibworth Beauchamp (inn GR 790968).

Although one of the longest walks in the book, this is one of the least demanding. The way is entirely along well-marked paths and trackways, most of the gradients are gentle, and there are very few stiles to negotiate. And the views are superlative.

The Walk
Cross the road and follow the lane (North End) directly opposite, climbing easily out of the village. After crossing a stream (by ford or by footbridge), go up the bank on the right to take a waymarked footpath, ascending steadily over vast 'prairie'-lands to reach the Midshires Way, on the ridge. At some times of the year, the path is clear and easy to follow, but with a crop in the field it can be difficult, particularly as the first field is extremely big and the distant stile invisible from the start – so you may perhaps prefer to remain with the track (Goadby Road), joining the Midshires Way a little to the south of the footpath.

Turn right along the Midshires Way, following the low ridge. At first the Way is no more than an unmade farmtrack, but after passing Keythorpe Lodge Farm, it graduates to become a metalled farm road. Pass the summit trig point (there is a good view ahead here of Keythorpe Hall) and descend to Keythorpe Hall Farm.

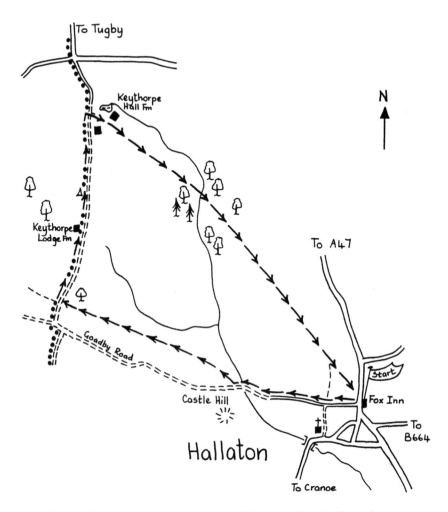

Turn right at the farm, leaving the Midshires Way. Follow the concrete farm road past the buildings and continue along a broad track. Some way on, the farm track bends right through a gateway, but the footpath keeps straight ahead over the field to rejoin the track at the far side. Here again, though, growing crops can be a problem, and you will perhaps be excused for following the track round.

Descend to cross a brook, climbing out again past new plantations, and leaving the farm track by a field path on the right, leading to a gate beside Moor Hill Spinney. Continue beside the wood and on over a succession of fields, alternating to right and left of the hedge.

On reaching a farm gate, the bridleway turns right, to follow the hedge down to Goadby Road, continuing on from there to reach the village church. This is the recommended route if, before completing your journey, you wish to see something of Hallaton itself. The more direct footpath route continues ahead, crossing this field and the next, over the 'rigg and furrow', to reach the road just by the Fox Inn.

Midshires Way – Cranoe to Tilton on the Hill (8½ miles)

The Way crosses the Hallaton road at Cranoe, climbing steeply. The village road is left on the bend by the church, the path continuing on the same line over the fields and following a low ridge. The route is undefined at first, but provided the wayfarer keeps to the highest ground and follows the regular Midshires Way waymarks carefully in a straight line there is little chance of going astray. From Goadby Road (little more than a farm road) to Keythorpe Hall Farm the route is as described in the above walk.

After passing Keythorpe Hall Farm, the lane descends to meet the Tugby public road, continuing on from here direct to Tugby (where there is the Fox and Hounds Inn).

Through Tugby, the route continues over the A47 trunk road, turning left before Tugby Wood and over the fields to Skeffington Gap. Immediately before reaching the road, it turns sharp right through a gate, following the hedge. From here the Way follows a direct line to Tilton on the Hill. The paths are mostly good, well waymarked – and have the additional advantage of Tilton's distant church spire to aim for.

[3]   Tilton on the Hill
The Rose and Crown

As the name suggests, Tilton occupies a superb hilltop site, with fine and extensive views. The village inn, the Rose and Crown, has a cheerful and friendly, old-world atmosphere, underlined by some interior stone walling, ancient beams, and a magnificent open fireplace in the cosy lounge bar. An intriguing feature is a collection of used film-props, including an ornate throne from *Robin Hood, Prince of Thieves*, one of Quasimodo's bells and a pair of Egyptian figures, too tall to stand erect, which gaze down menacingly from the ceiling!

This is an Ansells house and the ales on offer include Ansells Bitter, Tetley Bitter and Mild, and Bass. The ciderholic can choose from Taunton Dry or Sweet, or Addlestones Cask, or the lagers are Carlsberg, Pilsner, Castlemaine XXXX and Lowenbrau. Food is available throughout the opening times, and specialities include scampi, fillet of plaice, deep fried chicken and lasagne. There is a choice of salads, in addition to ploughman's lunch and jacket potatoes. The omelettes are especially recommended – and the servings are staggering. Light bites include filled rolls and toasted sandwiches. Families are welcome at the Rose and Crown, and there is both a family room and an outside children's play area, as well as a beer garden.

The hours of opening are from 12 noon to 3 pm and 6 pm to 11 pm in the week, and all day on Saturday and Sunday.
Telephone: 0116 2597234.

How to get there: Tilton on the Hill is situated beside the B6047 Melton Mowbray to Market Harborough road, about 2 miles north of the A47 Leicester to Uppingham trunk road (Billesdon bypass). The Rose and Crown is in the centre of the village, on the corner of Main Street and directly opposite the church.

Parking: Provided you are using the pub, you are welcome to leave your car here while taking your walk. Limited roadside parking is also possible.

Length of the walk: 5½ miles (shorter version of 5 miles possible). Maps: OS Landranger 141 Kettering and Corby, Pathfinder 895 Leicester East (inn GR 743057).

An interesting feature of the countryside around Tilton is its rich heritage of medieval village sites. This walk passes through one such site, in the course of a journey over gently rolling hills, presenting glorious views over many miles of north Leicestershire (and beyond).

The Walk
Follow Main Street through the village. Join the Midshires Way at a T-junction and turn right.

Continue round the bend, turning right again to follow Back Lane through to the B6047 road.

Turn left, and right again at the Houghton turning. After passing a house, on your right, leave the road by a farm gate on the right, waymarked for the Midshires Way, and follow the fence, with a barn on your left, over this field and the next. Continue around the end of this second field, following the hedge till you reach a dip, where the path turns right, through a farm gate. Go through, and keep straight forward over the field, making for a distant yellow-topped post.

Bear left at the post, and meet a farm track. Follow this along the hilltop, with a hedge on your left. There are extensive views here, ahead and to the right, including, in the far distance – when conditions are clear enough – the cooling towers of Ratcliffe on Soar power station, something like 35 miles further on along the Midshires Way.

Descend past Hamner's Lodge Farm and follow the metalled farm track through to the road, Skeg Hill. Turn right, then left onto the waymarked bridleway, following the line indicated by the guide-post. (If it is wet underfoot, bear left around the side of the field.)

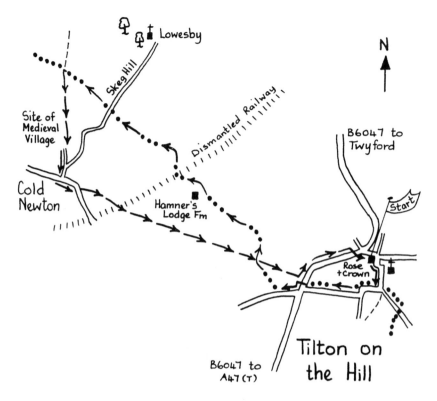

Follow the field's edge round to a handgate. Towards the end of the next field, leave the Midshires Way, turning left to cross a couple of stiles and a boggy patch.

Follow the ensuing path through a spinney. Cross a footbridge on the right and emerge once more on the open field. In the second field, cross a stile on the left and then go over the field on a diagonal line as indicated by the yellow arrow. This field is the site of the medieval village of Cold Newton, and the hummocky nature of its surface is ample evidence of the former dwellings. All is green now, the only occupants a flock of sheep. At the end of the field a farm gate leads out into the present village.

Follow the village street down to Hungarton Road and turn left. Where the road bends right, pass through a gate on your left and continue on the same line, following the left side of the hedge. In a second field bear left, to reach a stile.

Over the stile, descend and cross a disused railway track. Climbing out the other side, cross another stile and follow the hedge up the side

23

of the field. At the top, cross the wire fence via a stile and turn left onto a stone track.

Through the gate, continue with the track to a second gate. Leave the track here and continue straight ahead on the left of the hedge to reach a stream, crossed by a sturdy footbridge – and accessed by a very tricky stile and a slippery wet slope.

Go over the (much better) stile on the far side and continue up the ensuing fields, keeping towards the right. After crossing the line of the Midshires Way bear left, to pass through a gateway. Cross this field, passing to the right of a pond and a plantation, then go over a stile and a final field to reach the B6047. Cross over and follow the road back to Tilton.

Note: The above circuit can be shortened by ½ mile by turning left at Skeg Hill and rejoining the main route in Cold Newton village.

Midshires Way – Tilton on the Hill to Thimble Hall (5 miles)

The Midshires Way follows the route described in the pub walk, crossing over the road at Skeg Hill and continuing from here on the same line, initially with the hedge/fence on the left. After passing through a farm gate it goes on down the centre of two fields, bearing left in the second to reach Park Road, at the corner of a wood, by White's Barn.

Continuing through the wood, Inkerman Lodge is passed and the Way bears right over a field, keeping to the left of a hedge. After crossing two more fields the route turns right along the nearside of the hedge, continuing over the fields, mainly by the hedge, to reach Carr Bridge. This little hump-backed, cobblestoned bridge is today no more than a farm access between two fields. But its name and nature suggest that it – and the footpath – were once of far greater significance.

From Carr Bridge, the route follows the hedgeside through to the Leicester road at Thimble Hall, as described in Pub Walk 4.

[4] Twyford
The Saddle

The quiet village of Twyford nestles in the valley of the Gaddesby Brook, and the village pub, like most of the village, lies just off the main road on the unclassified lane to John o'Gaunt and Burrough on the Hill. The Saddle is one of Mansfield Brewery's houses, a cosy little traditional village pub, the décor of which reflects the equestrian flavour of its name, with saddles, horseshoes, brasses and prints. The main drinking area is the Stable Bar, and there is a separate, partitioned dining area. Ales include Mansfield Bitter and Riding Mild, and both Strongbow and Scrumpy Jack cider are served, as well as Foster's, Grolsch and Stella Artois lager. The wine list includes both French and German labels. Food is available throughout the hours of opening, except on Monday, the chef's day off. Last orders are taken half an hour before closing. The daily menu is posted up on the bar blackboard and may include prawn cocktail, scampi provençale, home-made lasagne, beef and kidney stew, swordfish or omelettes. For a not-so-light snack, try the superb and ginormous baguettes – with beef, ham, turkey or cheese. A ploughman's lunch is available with either Cheddar or Stilton. Specialities of the house are carveries on Sunday (lunch) and Thursday (evening) and regular 'Steak Nights'. Families are welcome at the Saddle, if dining. There is no beer garden as such, but there is an outside drinking area, and your dog will be welcome there.

On Monday to Saturday the opening times are from 11.30 am to 3 pm and 6 pm to 11 pm, and on Sunday from 12 noon to 3 pm and 7 pm to 10.30 pm.

Telephone: 01664 840237.

How to get there: The B6047 Melton Mowbray to Market Harborough road passes through Twyford. Turn south-east from the main road, heading for the parish church, opposite which is the Saddle inn.

Twyford is served by a Blands bus service between Grantham, Melton and Somerby.

Parking: We are assured that there is no objection to customers leaving their vehicles here for the duration of their walk, but note that space is very limited. For this reason, we suggest that it would be more considerate to leave your car on the roadside.

Length of the walk: 4³/₄ miles. Maps: OS Landranger 129 Nottingham and Loughborough and 141 Kettering and Corby, and Pathfinder 875 Melton Mowbray and Syston and 895 Leicester East (inn GR 730100).

This walk takes us first over fields, both grass and arable, to Lowesby Park, passing the site of the medieval village of Lowesby. From here we follow a valley path, close by the Queniborough Brook, to tiny Carr Bridge, where we join the Midshires Way. We return to Twyford past the quaintly-named Thimble Hall, following the road back from here to the village.

The Walk

Turn left out of the pub, following Main Street, to turn left again onto King Street. On the bend, just before the B6047, leave the road by a waymarked footpath on the left. Cross the first field and continue ahead over the succeeding fields, keeping to the direct line indicated by the waymark arrows. Careful navigation is necessary over these first fields as the route is lightly trodden and not always obvious. Pass close on the right of a pylon on the hilltop, continuing beside the hedge to a farm gate and stile.

From here, the path bears left to cross two fields on a diagonal line. Over the second field, climb the stile and turn right, following the fence beside two fields to reach the B6047, and cross over.

Follow the minor road opposite and enter the Lowesby Estate, keeping to the road as you descend over open parkland. The medieval village stood on ground to the left here, but nothing is evident from the

26

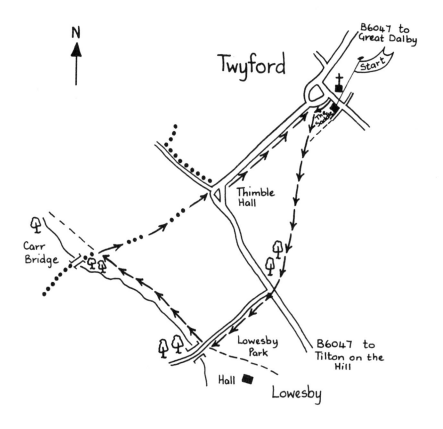

road, other than a suggestion of ridge and furrow, which itself is not uncommon hereabouts. The present village of Lowesby, and Lowesby Hall, can both be seen on the far side of the park.

Turn right at the bottom of the hill, following a field path to the right of a wood, to arrive at interesting little Carr Bridge. This is a particularly easy path to follow, with no stiles but farm gates all the way.

The Midshires Way is joined at Carr Bridge. Double back on yourself here, following the hedge on your left all the way to the Leicester road, at Thimble Hall.

Keep straight ahead over the road junction, joining the B6047, and follow the road down to Twyford. On reaching the village, take the first turning on the right – King Street – to return to the pub via your outward route.

27

Midshires Way – Thimble Hall to Gaddesby (5 miles)

At Thimble Hall, the way turns left along the road for ½ mile. It then turns right along a farm lane, passing Freezeland Lodge – apparently a retirement home for superannuated farm machinery! The lane emerges into a vast open field (ex-parkland?), bearing left a little to head for a distant belt of woodland, to the right of Ashby Folville Hall. After crossing a farm track, the Way continues ahead to reach a second farm track, where it turns right, following the track through to the road (B674) on the edge of Ashby Folville.

The route then turns left, following the road through the village (where there is the Carrington Arms Inn) and continuing, still on the B674, past the entrance to Ashby Folville Hall and on towards Gaddesby. The Way leaves the road at the Barsby turning, where a bridleway on the right takes over. From here to Gaddesby Lane, the route is as described in Pub Walk 5.

Carr Bridge.

28

[5] Gaddesby
The Cheney Arms

Gaddesby's lovely parish church, with its rich stonework and graceful spire, is home to one of Leicestershire's most striking and unusual monuments; an equestrian statue of the village's soldier hero, Colonel Cheney. The colonel who, reportedly, had no fewer than five horses shot from under him during the battle of Waterloo, is also commemorated in the title of the local hotel. A 17th-century dower house, the Cheney Arms is a large and welcoming hostelry with a friendly manager and staff. There are some massive old beams, a big open fireplace with copper warming pans beside it, hunting scenes upon the walls, and a particularly fearsome-looking 'ball on a rope' – to discourage potential trouble-makers?

Food is available throughout the opening hours. Starters include home-made Stilton soup and the pub's own pâté. For a main course you can select from, for example, breaded haddock or plaice, smoked salmon, half a roast chicken, home-made faggots and sirloin steak. If you fancy a ploughman's, you may opt for either Red Cheddar or Melton Stilton. There are also various daily specials on the blackboard. This is an Everards house and you will find a wide variety of ales, including Morland Old Speckled Hen and Adnams, alongside Old Original and

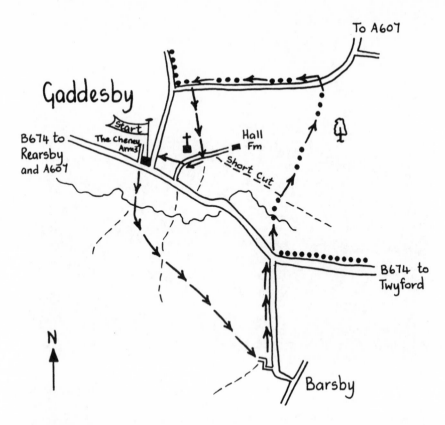

Gaddesby

B674 to
Rearsby
and A607

Start

The Cheney Arms

Hall Fm

Short Cut

To A607

B674 to Twyford

N

Barsby

Beacon. Draught cider is on offer and there are lagers by Carling and Budweiser, and wines, both red and white. Families are welcome here and there is a children's play area, as well as a beer garden. Overnight accommodation is available.

Lunchtime opening is from 12 noon to 2.30 pm on Monday to Friday and from 12 noon to 3 pm at the weekend. The Cheney Arms is open in the evenings from 5.30 pm to 11 pm on Monday to Saturday and from 7 pm to 10.30 pm on Sunday.

Telephone: 01664 840260.

How to get there: From the A607 Leicester to Melton road, turn east at Rearsby, following the B674 Twyford road. The village of Gaddesby is about 3 miles on, and the Cheney Arms stands on the corner, where the village road turns off left.

The A and S Travel bus service between Leicester and Rearsby calls here (not Sundays).

Parking: The Cheney Arms has its own roomy car park – but ask permission before leaving your wheels here while you walk.

Length of the walk: 4¹/₄ miles (shorter version of 3 miles possible). Maps: OS Landranger 129 Nottingham and Loughborough, and Pathfinder 875 Melton Mowbray and Syston (inn GR 687129).

Gaddesby lies in the pleasant, rolling, hunting shires country between Leicester and Melton Mowbray. There are some massive village churches hereabouts – those, for instance, at Gaddesby itself and its neighbour, Ashby Folville. The agriculture is mixed and you will encounter upon your journey both cattle and sheep, and cross an arable field or two.

The Walk
Turn right outside the pub, and immediately left, following the waymarked track between an avenue of trees. At the top of the avenue, cross a footbridge over a stream and bear left to reach a metal farm gate. Bear left again in the next field, passing through the gap and continuing on the same diagonal line to reach a stile, accessed via a slate footbridge over the ditch.

Over the stile, cross the field, making for a stile at the leftward end of a row of horse chestnut trees. The path as shown on the Pathfinder map bears slightly left of the hedge over the next two fields, but you may find (particularly if the field is cropped) that it has been diverted along the edge and around the end of the second field.

Cross the stile at the end of this second field and keep straight ahead, making for the farm buildings. Do not continue quite as far as these, however, but bear left to reach a stile beside a gate, leading into a rough lane. Follow the lane – which can be very muddy in season – to emerge onto the road by the King William Inn in the little village of Barsby.

Turn left and follow the road away from the village to reach the B674. Halfway down is a seat, where you may take a well-deserved rest.

Cross the B674 and join the Midshires Way. Bear left a little initially, following the hedge round in an arc to circumvent a low-lying area, and arrive at a narrow plank bridge. Beyond the bridge, the bridleway follows an enclosed route – impossible to go wrong – all the way through to the next road.

The pub walk can, however, be reduced to an overall distance of 3 miles by turning left onto a waymarked footpath and making for Gaddesby village church. When we surveyed the route, there was a prominent notice: 'Bull in Field', so we opted for discretion and continued along the enclosed way!

At the road turn left, following this quiet hilltop road and enjoying the fine views to the south over Gaddesby and beyond. Partway along, a pleasant little footpath meanders through a narrow strip of woodland alongside the road, offering a welcome alternative route.

At the entrance to Gaddesby turn left by the first houses, leaving the Midshires Way.

Follow the waymarked Leicestershire Round footpath, keeping straight ahead over the second field and bearing leftward of the farm gate to cross a stile and turn right into a narrow lane. Past the church, follow the metalled footway through to the road and turn left, back to the Cheney Arms.

Midshires Way – Gaddesby to Old Dalby (7½ miles)

The Way leaves Gaddesby by the Rotherby road. Just after passing Carlton Lodge Farm the road is forsaken in favour of a waymarked bridleway on the left. This crosses a series of fields on a direct line, passing between a spinney on the left and a belt of woodland on the right, to join a stony track and turn right.

The track bends right, adopting a more northerly line, which is maintained all the way to Brooksby, sometimes as a simple field path but mostly along clear roads and tracks. A tantalising feature of the view from here is the beckoning hills of Charnwood Forest, over to the west.

After passing Spinney Farm and Cottages, the A607 (Melton to Leicester) road is reached, via the Brooksby Agricultural College Nurseries.

The main road is crossed and the minor road opposite followed to Hoby, a pretty village with a tortuous main street – and a welcoming pub of its own, the Blue Bell.

Through Hoby, the road passes round a final bend before heading for Asfordby. Just after this bend, the road is left by a bridleway, left, crossing the field to meet the opposite hedge and follow it down to the field corner. A fenced-in hedgeside path is joined which leads gently up to a roughly wooded hilltop. From here the path bears left over the fields, passing to the left of Barn Farm before joining a further stretch of fenced-in hedgeside path. A final field is crossed to arrive, via the Shoby Poultry Farm, at the A6006 road.

The Way turns left, and right again into Shoby village, continuing on a quiet field road to Grimston (where there is the Black Horse). Here it turns left and follows the road out of the village. At a T-junction it turns left, and right again at the next turning. The second turning along from here – Longcliffe Lane – will bring the wayfarer to Old Dalby, and Debdale Hill, close to the Crown.

[6] Old Dalby
The Crown

Old Dalby is a most interesting village, close by which the site of a Roman station has been located. The Old Hall had connections with the Knights Templars – and was also, at one time, the home of the notorious Judge Jeffreys.

The Crown is a freehouse, and a hidden gem – this author circled the village three times before he found it! Unlike many of our village inns, this one was built as such, round about the end of the 16th century. The atmosphere is fantastic, with tiny, cosy little rooms, comfy seats, and an open coal fire on cold days. The old-fashioned bar has a collection of casks stacked behind the counter, offering an extensive assortment of real ales – Marston's Pedigree and Best, Kimberley, Adnams, Abbot Ale, Wherry, Nelson's Revenge, Moonraker, Cains, London Pride and Old Speckled Hen, to name but a few. The décor includes a set of humorous prints of the hunt, off duty, as well as a picture of the inn when it resembled, even more closely than it does today, a working farmhouse. And the exterior aspect is equally attractive.

As well as the vast range of ales, the liquid refreshment on offer includes Strongbow cider, Carlsberg Hof lager, and a choice of 35 wines. Food is available throughout opening times. There are various starters and light appetizers, as well as steak and rabbit pie, Crown grill, New Hampshire pot roast, rack of lamb, pan-fried escalope of salmon and French duck breast. Vegetarians are catered for too and there is a selection of home-made puddings. If all you require is a snack, there are a number of different sandwiches and rolls to pick from. Families are welcome. Accommodation includes a family room and a children's play area, a beer garden and a non-smoking zone. Dogs are allowed inside, if on a lead.

Lunchtime opening is from 12 noon to 3 pm each day. The evening times are from 6 pm to 11 pm except Sunday, when the pub is open from 7 pm to 10.30 pm.

Telephone: 01664 823134.

How to get there: Old Dalby is best approached from the A46 (Foss Way) or the A606 Nottingham to Melton road. In either case, leave by the unclassified road running between the Willoughby Hotel (on the A46) and Upper Broughton (on the A606). About $1/2$ mile from the Willoughby Hotel turn south-east, and $11/2$ miles further on a turning on the left will bring you to the outskirts of Old Dalby. Look carefully for Debdale Hill on your right – it is a narrow residential road and easily missed. Turn down here and the Crown is directly ahead of you.

Bus services between Nottingham and Melton Mowbray call at Old Dalby (Bartons and Road Car).

Parking: Customers may park here while walking.

Length of the walk: $41/4$ miles. Maps: OS Landranger 129 Nottingham and Loughborough, and Pathfinder 854 Scalford and Nether Broughton (inn GR 671239).

A walk of wide views to east and west as we follow the line of the Midshires Way along the crest of Longcliffe Hill and over the county boundary into Nottinghamshire. We follow the road into Upper Broughton, returning to our starting point over quiet field paths beside the Dalby Brook.

The Walk
Cross the front of the pub and follow the road steeply uphill. It is perhaps a little early to be thinking of a rest, but a wayside seat is a timely reminder to pause for a moment and enjoy the view back over the village. Pass through a farm gate and continue round with the road to reach a second gate, leading out onto Longcliffe Lane. Cross the road and take the waymarked bridleway (the Midshires Way route) following the right-hand side of the hedge.

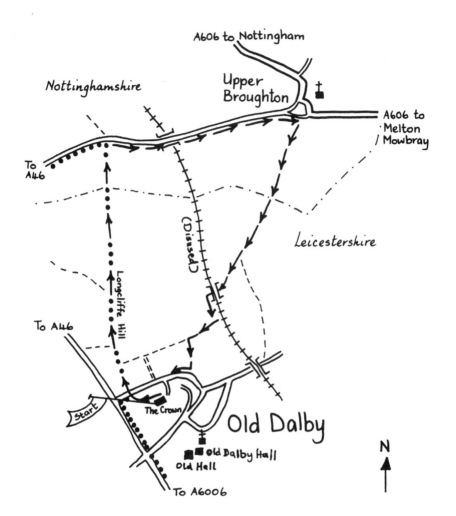

A606 to Nottingham

Nottinghamshire

Upper Broughton

A606 to Melton Mowbray

To A46

(Disused)

Leicestershire

Longcliffe Hill

To A46

Start

The Crown

Old Dalby

Old Dalby Hall

Old Hall

To A6006

N

Keep to the right of the hedge, enjoying the wide-ranging views over the Vale of Belvoir to the east, until you reach a farm gate. Pass through and follow the field boundary round to continue, now with the hedge on your right and the open views over to the left. Remain with this clear track, following the field boundary on the same south/north line, through to the Upper Broughton road.

Turn right, and continue to Upper Broughton. Just short of the village, a welcome seat on the left offers the opportunity for a brief rest. Where the road branches keep right, following the Top Green road. Leave by a stile (easily missed) on the right, almost opposite the Old Saddlery.

Cross one small field, then a second, larger one, from corner to corner, with the farm buildings to your right. Cross a third field, still following the same diagonal line, and turning half-right over a stile to follow the fence down to a footbridge over a brook.

Over the bridge, turn left along the side of the stream. Cross another stile and bear right over two fields to reach a plantation, and Dalby Brook. Follow the brook, keeping the stream on your left and crossing a stile, before continuing, still on the right of both brook and hedge, until you reach a waymark pointing left through a gap. Go through and continue, now on the left of the stream, to reach the railway embankment, passing through under a bridge.

Turn left, following the waymarked route beside the hedge and the railway. Turn right with the trodden route, beside a ditch, and follow the hedge for the length of one field. At the top, turn left over a stile and follow the path around two sides of the field, heading first for the houses on the outskirts of Old Dalby, then right, to the Longcliffe Lane. Keep forward along the road, to reach Debdale Hill on your left.

Midshires Way – Old Dalby to Wysall (6 miles)

The Way follows the pub walk route from Longcliffe Lane to the Upper Broughton road. At this point it turns left, keeping to the road, passing the Willoughby Hotel and crossing the Foss Way, to reach Willoughby on the Wolds. There are three successive turnings on the right, all leading to Willoughby. The Midshires Way takes the third of these.

The equestrian route follows the road from here to Wysall, but there is a footpath alternative for the walker. This leaves the road via a stile on the left at the extreme end of the village (West Thorpe).

The path crosses the field diagonally, descending to a stile close to the opposite corner. Crossing the stile, it adopts a line to the right of the Kingston Brook, following the route taken by Pub Walk 7 from here to Wysall church.

[7]   Wysall
The Plough

There can be few more charming examples of a genuine traditional
country inn than this 300 year old freehouse, set in the pretty south
Nottinghamshire village of Wysall. The staff are friendly and welcoming,
the atmosphere cosy and relaxed. There are old beams and brassware
– including brass pistols behind the bar – and a lovely open fireplace
complements the tiled floor. But the feature that first catches the eye is
the beautiful setting of the house, with its delightful beer garden a joy
at any time, and second to none when the flowers are in full bloom.

Speciality ales include Bass Pedigree, Tetley and various guest beers.
The cider is Dry Blackthorn and the lager drinker can choose either
Carling Black Label or Tennent's Extra. There are also various wines
to tickle your palate. Food is available daily from 12 noon to 2.15 pm,
although on Sunday this is restricted to hot beef cobs. From Monday to
Saturday the full selection includes Grandma Batty's delicious Yorkshire
puddings with a choice of fillings, chicken dishes, vegetable curry and
a tasty ploughman's lunch. Families are welcome, although there is no
separate family room or any play area. But there is that splendid garden
– and no objection to patrons eating their own snap there when food is
not otherwise available. Well-behaved dogs are also welcome.

The Plough is open from 12 noon to 3 pm and 7 pm to 10.30 pm on Sunday and from 12 noon to 4 pm and 6 pm to 11 pm in the week. Saturday has all-day opening, from 12 noon through to 11 pm.
Telephone: 01509 880339.

How to get there: From the A60 Nottingham to Loughborough road, turn off east at either Costock or Bradmore, following the signposts for Wysall. The Plough stands in an elevated position, on the eastern side of the road at the northern end of the village.

The Nottingham to Leicester bus service (Bartons) passes through Wysall.

Parking: The inn has its own car park across the road, which you are welcome to use while taking your walk. Roadside parking is also possible in the village.

Length of the walk: 4¹/₂ miles. Maps: OS Landranger 129 Nottingham and Loughborough, and Pathfinder 854 Scalford and Nether Broughton (inn GR 605274).

The villages of Willoughby and Wysall are the first in Nottinghamshire to be met on the Midshires Way. The equestrian route follows the road between the two, so the walker has the advantage of pleasant field paths untouched by the less desirable effects of horse traffic. This easy-walking route passes close to the site of the Civil War battle of Willoughby Field, and the lost medieval village of Thorpe in the Glebe.

The Walk
Follow Main Street south from the Plough, turning left on the bend by the village church onto the Wymeswold road. Keep to the road, passing the 'Thorpe in the Glebe' sign and continuing to the top of the rise. Leave the road here by a waymarked bridleway on the left, opposite Windyridge Farm.

Follow the track along the side of the field. At the end of the second field, the track leaves the fields via a metal gate. There is a 'Private' sign here but we are assured by the Nottinghamshire County Council that there is a right of way along the track. So continue, passing the Frank Hind Field Centre (Nottingham and Notts Field Club) to arrive at a second gate. This one may be chained up, but can be passed via a gap on one side or a makeshift stile on the other. Keep on over two fields, passing the end of an overgrown track in the third and swinging left to reach Woodside Farm.

Turn right at the farm, with your back to the stile, following the overhead wires to a gate beside a wood. Walk alongside the edge of the

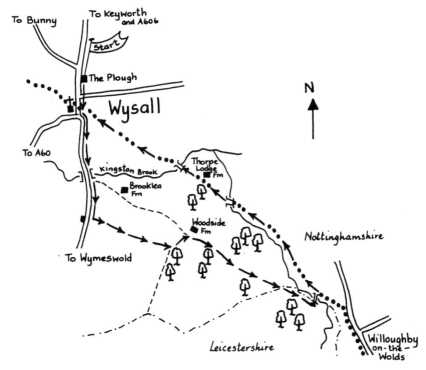

wood, bearing right at the end to cross a stile and turn left along the side of the hedge. At the end of this field, turn left over a stile and footbridge (or through the gap) and continue along the left of Triangle Plantation. After the wood, follow the hedge on your left down one field, then over a second field, corner to corner. Go down a third field, again following the hedge to a gate. Pass through and continue on through the gap by a tall pylon. Turn left, joining the Midshires Way.

Follow the Midshires Way path in a straightish line over many fields, with the Kingston Brook close at hand on the left. After crossing the third intervening lane, cross the stream and continue diagonally over a very large field, passing between a wood on the left and Thorpe Lodge Farm on your right. Cross a difficult stile (a pair of secateurs might be useful!) and continue on a clear track, negotiating two right-angles in the hedgeline to recross the brook and turn left.

The Way from here again follows a fairly straight route, all the way back to Wysall. If you can make out the spire of Wysall church among the trees in front, you have a useful waymark. After crossing (or circumnavigating, if there is a growing crop) a very large field, negotiate another stile and follow the fence ahead. Towards the end, bear right a little and cross a paddock, then go over fields to reach Wysall's Main Street, outside the village hall.

Turn right for the pub.

Midshires Way – Wysall to West Leake (9½ miles)

The Midshires Way again offers a choice of routes between Wysall and Bunny, with two alternatives for the rider and a third option for the walker. This one leaves the village street by an enclosed passageway on the left as you walk from the church – opposite the Old Post Office and next to Keeper's Lodge. Reaching the fields, the route crosses the first from corner to corner, continuing half-left to follow the hedge on a more westerly line over three fields. A concealed stile in the second leads through the hedge at one point. There are fine views over to the left here, in the direction of Loughborough.

The way turns right opposite a wood – Rough Plantation – and continues northward over the next two fields. It then crosses two fields on a diagonal line to reach Bunny Old Wood Nature Reserve. If there is a growing crop in the larger field, it may be found that the path has been diverted around the edge.

The path descends through the wood to meet the main riders' route and turns left to follow the bridleway through to the main A60 road. Here it turns right, down Bunny Hill, and left again onto Gotham Lane. The Rancliffe Arms is worth a diversion while in the Bunny area.

Past Welldale Farm, the way turns left into Taft Leys Lane, a pleasant green lane which climbs steadily up to a height of 92 metres (302 ft). No Everest, but all these things are relative, and the views from the top are splendid – behind over the Trent Valley and the City of Nottingham, and ahead, in the descent, to Charnwood Forest.

The track turns right after Taft Leys Farm and continues to East Leake and the Gotham road. The route turns right again along the road, crossing the railway (now derelict) and on up the unclassified road directly in front. Past the Rushcliffe (Golf) Club House the track swings left, following a scenic route over Fox Hill and on to West Leake village. Then the Way is along the village street, turning left at the end, and right again at Melton Lane, to reach the Star Inn.

[8] West Leake
The Star

West Leake, a pretty little village nestling at the foot of the Leake hills and close to Kingston Brook, is a quiet, unspoilt, unassuming place, with charming footpath walks in every direction – and a welcoming inn for thirsty (or hungry) travellers. First recorded as an alehouse in 1750, the Star's local name is the Leake Pit House, which we are told has nothing to do with mineral extraction, but with a cock pit – a clear indication of the form of 'entertainment' popular hereabouts in days gone by. A much more desirable establishment today, the cosy bar-room boasts a welcoming coal fire in season, with brass fire-irons, and other brass and copperware on the mantelshelf. There are ancient beams above and tiled floors below, high-backed settles and comfortable chairs and stools, and an interesting collection of old jugs and bottles on the high shelves. This is a relaxed and friendly country pub where total strangers greet you with a cheery word.

Food is available every lunchtime. The menu varies from day to day in the week, with a different selection at weekends. Depending when you call, you may find ploughman's or dairyman's platter, or fisherman's catch. Or there may be, for example, chicken Madras, baked salmon steaks or Lincolnshire sausage. Afters include banana split, peach melba and bread and butter pudding. Vegetarian dishes are available, and, for the light biter, delicious filled rolls. The ales on offer include Bass and Theakston XB. There are lagers by Carling and Beck's, and the cider is Strongbow. Families are welcome, and will find a separate family room as well as a children's play area. There is also a beer garden. Well-behaved dogs are welcome too.

Lunchtime opening is from 11 am to 2.30 pm on Monday to Friday, extended to 3.30 pm on Saturday, and from 12 noon to 3 pm on Sunday. The evening times are from 6 pm to 11 pm on Monday to Saturday, and 7 pm to 10.30 pm on Sunday.

Telephone: 01509 852233.

How to get there: From the A453 (M1 link), turn off south by the Ratcliffe on Soar power station, or from the A60, turn west at Costock, passing through the larger settlement of East Leake, to arrive, in either case, at the much smaller village of West Leake. At the western end of the village street turn south, then go right at the Sutton Bonington turning. The pub is just around this corner, on the right.

There is an occasional bus (Soar Valley) between here and Loughborough.

Parking: The pub has a large car park, which you are welcome to use while following the walk.

Length of the walk: 5¼ miles (or 4¼ miles if you take the short cut, omitting West Leake village street). Maps: OS Landranger 129 Nottingham and Loughborough, and Pathfinder 853 Loughborough North (inn GR 524262).

The first mile and a half of this walk follows the route of the Midshires Way, to the outskirts of Sutton Bonington. We visit also the charming village of Kingston on Soar, from where we return to West Leake via a delightful brookside field path, passing close to the imposing home of Lord Belper. A short cut back to the pub is possible but it would be a pity not to finish the walk with a circuit of this pretty little village.

The Walk

Turn right from the pub, following the Midshires Way route along Melton Lane. This is an unclassified road, with no footpath for most of the way, and it can be very busy, so keep well in to the right, using the grass verge as far as possible. This road is followed for about 1½ miles, to reach a crossroads on the outskirts of Sutton Bonington. Features to look out for along the way include the prominent cooling towers, over to your right, of Ratcliffe power station, and, on the left by the crossroads, the land and buildings of the Nottingham University

School of Agriculture. You may well also see one or two planes coming in to land at the nearby East Midlands Airport.

Leave the Midshires Way at the crossroads, turning right towards Kingston on Soar. You are still following the road, but here there is a footpath for your greater convenience. The busy Midlands to St Pancras rail line can be seen over to the left.

On reaching the pretty village of Kingston on Soar, with its charming little church of St Winifred, turn right over a stile, bearing right around the field to reach the Kingston Brook, opposite a picnic site, and with fine views of Kingston Hall, the family home of Lord Belper. Keep to the streamside, with occasional tantalising glimpses of the lake (The Pool) through the trees on your left. Leaving the parkland, the path continues, still beside the brook, over arable fields.

Cross the brook via a sturdy footbridge and go over the corner of the field to reach and cross a stile, returning to follow the brookside to a farm track. Turn left and follow the track up the field, swinging right with it to pass Scotland Farm. Keep the farm buildings on your left and swing right again to pass through a farm gate. Then turn left again, still following the track, and continue through to the road at West Leake, where the Midshires Way is rejoined.

A short cut back to the pub follows the road to the right here, but the village of West Leake is well worth exploring further. The main route continues straight ahead (following the Midshires Way, but in reverse) for the length of the village, passing another small but interesting

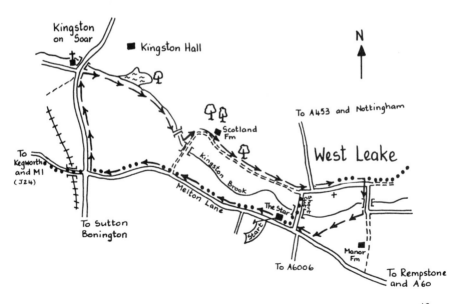

43

church. At the end of the village the road turns right, now following an alternative section of the Midshires Way, to cross the Kingston Brook and reach a gated farm track on the next bend. Through the gate, turn right over a stile, leaving the Midshires Way once more.

Follow the fence on the left of the field, then go straight over a second very large field to reach a mature shelter belt of trees. Walk through the trees, by a footbridge and a following stile, then go over one small field to the road. Turn right for the pub.

Midshires Way – West Leake to Shardlow Wharf (7½ miles)

The route between West Leake and Shardlow touches three counties, and is full of interest. The Way initially follows the route described in the pub walk, continuing ahead at the Sutton Bonington crossroads and passing the Station Inn, to reach the river Soar. Crossing the river bridge the wayfarer, back in Leicestershire for a while, enters the little town of Kegworth (where there is the Anchor Inn).

The route turns right, following Long Lane out of the town and crossing the A453. After negotiating a series of bends, the Way continues along a waymarked bridleway on the right, following a telegraph line over several fields to reach a metalled lane leading to the B6540 road, by Sawley Marina.

Turning right here, the Way joins the towpath of the Sawley Cut, on the left, continuing as described in Pub Walk 9, to Shardlow, in Derbyshire.

[9] Shardlow
The New Inn

Shardlow's main claim to fame rests on its situation at the very beginning of the Trent and Mersey Canal. The wharf, with its adjacent stretches of canal, is lively and colourful, with a variety of watercraft and wildfowl, anglers – and a couple of excellent pubs. The New Inn is a busy and popular wharfside hostelry, dating back to the late 18th century. The house has grown in size over the years, but still retains the same cheerful and friendly atmosphere. And we have it on the very best authority (that of the proprietor) that ramblers are especially welcome.

This is a Bass Tavern, offering Bass, Worthington and a variety of guest ales. Cider is Red Rock and Dry Blackthorn, and lagers include Carling, Tennent's and Grolsch. There is a selection of French and German wines. Food is available every day from noon until 2 pm. Everything is home cooked and the menu changes daily. Specialities include fresh fish, the Sunday lunches and the delicious hot filled cobs. Families are welcome, and the lawn area makes a popular children's play area in the summer. Dogs, if well-behaved, are also welcome.

The inn is open all day – on Monday to Saturday from 11 am through to 11 pm, and on Sunday from 12 noon until 10.30 pm.

Telephone: 01332 792310.

How to get there: Shardlow village is on the A6 trunk road, between Derby and the M1, and just north of the river Trent at Cavendish Bridge. Leave the main road at the eastern end of the village, by the Navigation Inn, following Wilne Lane. Cross the canal bridge, and turn left onto the wharf. The New Inn is on the right, the first of two pubs on the wharf.

A jointly operated bus service between Derby, Loughborough and Leicester calls at Shardlow.

Parking: There is no objection to genuine customers parking here and walking, but adequate alternative facilities are available just a stone's throw away (Shardlow Wharf car park).

Length of the walk: 4$\frac{1}{2}$ miles (or a shorter alternative of 2$\frac{1}{4}$ miles). Maps: OS Landranger 129 Nottingham and Loughborough, and Pathfinder 833 Nottingham South-West (inn GR 445306).

This is a walk of infinite variety, in two counties, beginning with a stroll by quiet country lanes and footpaths to touch the small township of Sawley. We twice cross the M1 motorway – once over and the second time under. And we make the acquaintance of two famous rivers and one equally famous canal.

The Walk

Leaving the New Inn, turn left onto Wilne Lane and continue through Great Wilne – a tiny village with delusions of grandeur! Beyond the village, at the end of the lane, cross two stiles and turn right, following the footpath over a large field to reach a footbridge over the river Derwent.

For the shorter walk, turn right before the bridge and follow an easy field path, initially by the riverside, to Derwent Mouth Lock, where you rejoin the main walk on the south side of the canal. But be warned – there is no footbridge, the only option when we came being to cross via the lock-gates. There is a hand-rail, but this route is not likely to appeal if you suffer from vertigo!

For the main walk, cross the footbridge and, on reaching the lane, turn right, leaving the Midshires Way after $\frac{1}{4}$ mile as it branches off left onto a field path.

Continue along the lane, through to the Draycott road. As you follow the lane you will have your first glimpse of the spire of Sawley church and – rather more prominent – the cooling towers of Ratcliffe power station, all on your right.

At the junction with the Draycott road – opposite the Church Wilne Treatment Works – turn right, crossing over the M1. Continue through

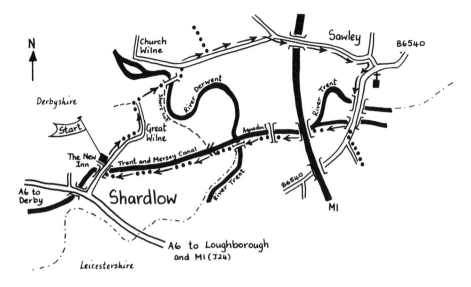

to the outskirts of Sawley. Immediately after a sharp turn left, by Bothe Hall, turn right into an unmarked passageway between a white building and an old red-brick wall. This follows a winding route for some distance, between walls, to emerge onto more open ground at Bothe Hall Meadow and reach the road. Turn right, now on the B6540, and follow the road over the river Trent and, for a wee while, back into Leicestershire. Take care crossing the bridge – the footway is narrow in places and, despite its secondary numbering, this is a busy road.

At Sawley Cut, opposite the marina, the Midshires Way is rejoined. Turn right and follow the towing path on the left of the waterway. From here to Shardlow the quality of the walk – and it was good before – improves immeasurably, with the varied attractions of wildfowl, river and canal-craft, and patient anglers on the waterways and adjacent ponds, a constant delight.

The cut opens out into the river Trent, where the path passes beneath, first, the motorway, and then an aqueduct, to reach Long Horse Bridge – which used to be just that, a long, arching bridge just broad enough in the beam to accommodate a canal horse. Cross the bridge, now part of the footpath network, and reach a form of 'crossroads'.

Three waterways meet at Long Horse Bridge. The river Trent takes a right-angled turn here from a northern to an eastern flow. On the north side of the cross is the mouth of the river Derwent. And on the west is the beginning of the Trent and Mersey Canal. This we shall follow, back in Derbyshire again.

Soon after joining the canal, the Derwent Mouth Lock is reached. This

47

is the first lock on the Trent and Mersey – and, at 90 ft, the longest on any British waterway. Pause here and, if you are lucky, you will be able to enjoy the activity as the lock-gates are put through their paces for the passing traffic.

Pass under Porter's Bridge, and continue on to the Wilne Lane Bridge, where the road is rejoined, just by Shardlow Wharf.

Midshires Way – Shardlow Wharf to Stanley (10 miles)
The Midshires Way follows the main pub walk route, through Great Wilne and over the fields and footbridge, to Wilne Lane, Sawley. After following the road for about 1/4 mile, a broad ash-track is reached, on the left. A stile to the right of this track gives access to the footpath, running parallel to it and continuing along the top of the flood bank to reach a lane, close to the river Derwent. The road is soon left again, via a footpath on the right beside a large square building, leading to Draycott (Coach and Horses), where it turns right onto Station Road.

The Way leaves Draycott via Town End Road, passing the Victoria Mills and bearing left over the railway to join and follow a country lane, which is soon left by a stile on the right. The way continues over the fields, generally on a diagonal line, and passing to the left of Cottage Farm, to join the road just outside Risley. The road is then followed, under the A52, to turn left onto the B5010.

A waymarked bridleway, opposite the Blue Ball, leads by a farm lane past Manor Farm to a wood. A path here leads off left, following the hedge over two fields, before turning left over a footbridge and continuing ahead over the fields to Constitution Hill. Here the Way leaves the broad plain of the Trent valley to head north-west into the Peak District. This is a good place to pause and look back, over the river Trent and away to the distant hills of Charnwood – and to say a last farewell to Ratcliffe on Soar power station, which has been a prominent landmark for many miles along the way. Then face about and set a course for Stockport.

Descending to Hopton Hall Farm, the Way turns right to follow clear paths and lanes, past Keys Farm, to the road at Sandiacre Lodge, continuing on along the road towards Dale. A footpath on the left bypasses the site of Dale Abbey, the solitary remaining arch of which can be seen below on the right, and leads to Hermit's Wood, where a run of steps on the left will lead to the 12th-century hermit's cave. From here the Way follows the route of Pub Walk 10 – past Columbine Farm to the A6096, turning right by Locko Park Gates to cross the fields to Stanley.

[10] Stanley
The White Hart

The village of Stanley (not to be confused with Stanley Common, a mile to the north), is tucked away in a maze of winding roads about halfway between Ilkeston and Derby and convenient to both. Originally a hunting lodge, the White Hart first became licensed premises in the late 18th century. The inn was sympathetically renovated about 1980, one of its most striking features being the welcoming log fire in the comfortable lounge on cold days. Another interesting touch is a number of cartwheels incorporated into the décor. On a more down-to-earth level this is the first pub we have visited where the human penchant for writing on lavatory walls is turned into an art form. The graffiti here are the most diverse – and tasteful – we have come across!

This is an Ansells house, offering Draught Burton Ale and Marston's Pedigree, Gaymer's Olde English Cider, and Skol, Carlsberg Export and Castlemaine XXXX lagers. Wines include draught French Auberge and Liebfraumilch. Food is available daily from noon until 2 pm. The Sunday menu consists of filled rolls only, but on other days you may choose from, among other dishes, gammon and pineapple, seafood platter, king rib of pork, moussaka, deep-fried plaice and steak and kidney pie, not to mention various salads and sweets. There is also a special children's menu. Families are welcome here and there is a family room and a play area. Well-behaved dogs are also welcome.

The opening hours are from 11 am to 3 pm and 7 pm to 11 pm on Monday to Saturday and from 12 noon to 3 pm and 7 pm to 10.30 pm on Sunday.

Telephone: 0115 9325048.

How to get there: From the A609 Ilkeston to Belper road, turn off south at Stanley Common (ie, at the western end of West Hallam), following the unclassified Stanley road. Turn right at a T-junction to arrive at Stanley village and follow the road round to reach the White Hart, facing you across the bend of Derby Road.

Stanley is served by buses between Derby and Ilkeston (Felix) and Derby, Ilkeston and Mansfield (Trent).

Parking: If patronising the pub, you are welcome to use the car park for the duration of your walk.

Length of the walk: 4$\frac{1}{2}$ miles. Maps: OS Landranger 129 Nottingham and Loughborough, and Pathfinder 833 Nottingham South-West and 812 Nottingham North and Ilkeston (inn GR 417403).

The high spot of this walk is a visit to the ancient village of Dale, once the home of an abbey and a hermitage. Both sites can be visited in the course of the journey.

The Walk

Turn right from the pub, following Derby Road as far as the Bridge Inn, and turning left here into Dale Road. Follow the clear track and its succeeding bridlepath to Lower Hagg Farm, where a new lane is joined. Pass Upper Hagg Farm and reach the A6096 Derby to Ilkeston road.

Cross the main road and follow Arbour Hill, turning right at the Carpenters Arms to arrive at the village of Dale Abbey.

This is a tiny place and a little off the beaten track, but it lacks nothing in interest. As you follow the village street, look out on your left for the single mighty arch which is now the only visible reminder of the once proud abbey. Further along, past the little church, a footpath on the left (off our route, but worth a diversion) leads to a hermit's cave. We are told that this was the retreat of a former Derby baker who, having received a vision of the Virgin Mary, came to Dale and founded the abbey. The village church, too, is a particularly attractive little building. There is a story – possibly apocryphal – that one end of the building used to be an inn, with a serving hatch through which the landlord could serve the vicar with a pint. Continuing past the church, the Midshires Way is

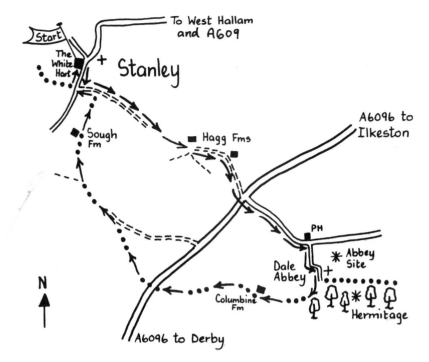

joined as it emerges from Hermit's wood.

Do not enter the wood, but keep straight ahead, following a clear track up and round over the wooded Dale Hills and passing to the left of Columbine Farm. Keep to this same track until, just before reaching the A6096, a footpath is met on the left of the lane. This leads direct to the road.

Cross the road to the gates of Locko Park – but do not enter. The Midshires Way turns right outside the gates, joining a field path. This goes straight over two fields, passing through a gateway on the right at the end, then immediately left again into a green lane. Keep straight forward and follow the lane to its end, then go round the edge of the next field. Follow the fence on the right of another field and continue over the fields, passing to the right of Sough Farm, to reach Dale Road. Turn left for Derby Road and Stanley village.

Midshires Way – Stanley to Blackbrook (10 miles)

This stage of the Way reaches a new landmark, the entry into stone wall country. Crossing the road from the Bridge Inn, the route follows well-marked field paths to Whitehouse Farm, where it turns left along a minor road, continuing by lanes and field paths to Morley. At the

51

A608 road, a left turn followed almost immediately by a compensating right turn leads to a farm lane. After passing the mysterious Morley Mound (a defensive motte?) the way continues to Morley Moor.

Crossing the road, the path bears right over the hill, turning left again at Priory Cottages and right by the entrance to the Breadsall Priory Golf Course. It continues over the golf course (beware of low – or high – flying missiles) and descends through woodland to a stony track, where it turns left.

The way passes the rear entrance to Drum Hill Scout Camp, then bears right along a side path, passing beneath the A38 and crossing the B6179 and a single-track railway (which, from the condition of the rails, appears to be still in use, so take care). It then turns left along Alfreton Road, and right again, after the Bell and Harp, climbing steeply up Whittaker Lane. This takes the Way up onto an old packhorse route, which is followed through woodland, over the ensuing fields and down a stepped path to reach Duffield Bridge (where there is the Bridge Inn).

The designated route to Duffield turns left over the bridge, crossing the fields to the church, then turning right over the footbridge to follow the field path alongside the railway and join the A6 road in Duffield.

The road is followed through Duffield, and is left after Castle Hill by a waymarked path on the corner of Avenue Road. The service road is followed past the (Chevin Golf Club) club house until this emerges onto open links. The way turns left here, following a field path round to a broad green track and climbing over a large field, after which it goes up through woods on the right to reach the ancient Portway track (North Lane) over the Chevin, where it turns left. The track is followed to the road at Farnah Green (where there is the Bluebell Inn Restaurant). Here it turns right, then left again by the post box. Thence the Way continues by field and woodland paths, and a stony lane to reach the A517 at Blackbrook.

[11] Shottlegate
The Hanging Gate

Shottlegate is a tiny crossroads hamlet situated at the intersection of the Belper to Ashbourne road with the winding minor road between Duffield and Wirksworth Moor. The Hanging Gate stands apart from the village, on the Belper side; a traditional country inn, parts of which are understood to date back to the early 16th century. There are time-honoured beams and flagged floors, and open coal fires in the winter. This is a Bass house, where the ales include Highgate and guest beers, as well as Carling and Tennent's lagers and Dry Blackthorn cider. An extensive choice of wines includes bottles from France, Australia, New Zealand and the USA.

The service is warm and friendly, and food is available throughout opening hours, with a wide selection of starters and main courses – fish, chicken and red meat dishes, pies, grills and salads. There is a tempting range of delicious sweets, and snacks include cheese and pickle ploughman's, pork pie ploughman's and massive sandwiches. Vegetarians are catered for too, and many of the dishes can be obtained in smaller portions, at reduced cost, for the kiddies. Families are welcome and will find a family room and a children's play area, as well as a beer garden and a non-smoking zone. Dogs are also welcome, but in the outside areas only.

The pub is open all day and every day in the summer from 11 am to 11 pm. The winter Monday to Wednesday hours are 12 noon to 3 pm and 5.30 pm to 11 pm and on Thursday to Sunday from 12 noon to 10.30 pm.
Telephone: 01773 550363.

How to get there: The pub is situated on the A517 road between Belper and Ashbourne. The road climbs steeply out of Belper until it reaches Blackbrook, where it levels out. The Hanging Gate is about ½ mile further, on the north side of the road.

Shottlegate can be reached by buses from Ashbourne and Belper (Stevensons) as well as from Derby and Matlock (Trent).

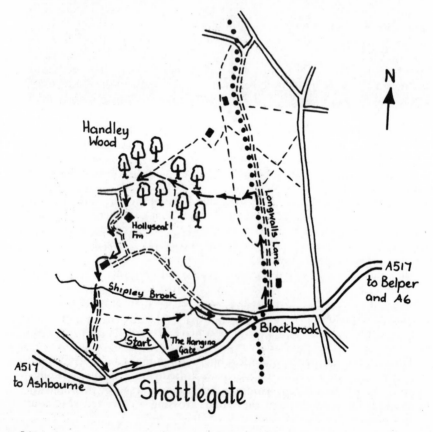

Parking: The pub has its own spacious car park, which you are welcome to use while walking.

Length of the walk: 4 miles. Maps: OS Landranger 119 Buxton and Matlock, and Pathfinder 811 Belper (inn GR 324474).

Between Duffield and Belper Lane End, the Midshires Way follows the route of the Old Portway, almost certainly the oldest road in Derbyshire. Here, to the west of the busy town of Belper, we get our first taste of the rolling hills and dry-stone walls of the Peak District. We follow the Portway along ancient Longwalls Lane, returning to base by way of quiet lanes, woods and field paths.

The Walk
Cross a stile in the far corner of the pub car park (beside the children's play area) and cross the ensuing field to reach a concealed stile and footbridge in the extreme left-hand corner. The bridge is a somewhat Heath-Robinson affair, crossing a ditch, so take care. Bear right a little in the next field to arrive at a squeezer beside a metal field gate.

Cross the next field, passing to the right of a row of trees, turning right by a free-standing pair of stone uprights, and cross a stile/squeezer into the next field. Continue straight down the field, passing to the right of a tree and bearing right to cross a footbridge over a stream, and on to join a lane.

Turn right and follow Plains Lane past Chapel House Farm, and the sad remains of the old chapel – now serving as a barn – continuing past a row of modern residences to rejoin the Belper to Ashbourne road. Turn left here, then left again on reaching the hamlet of Blackbrook and Longwalls Lane.

At Longwalls Lane we join the Midshires Way, which here follows the course of the Old Portway, one of the oldest roads in Derbyshire. It remains an unmetalled, wild country way, better adapted to walkers and horse-riders than to the motorised fraternity. The way climbs steeply, initially metalled and built up, but after passing the last of the houses it reverts to a pleasant tree-lined bridleway.

After a steep ascent in a hollow way the path levels out a little. Where a footpath crosses left to right, take the left turn through a squeezer, leaving the Midshires Way.

Follow the right of the wall over two fields. Pass to the left of a pond and turn right to reach a squeezer on your left.

Through the squeezer, continue straight down the middle of the field, and at the end of a second field cross a difficult stile to enter Handley Wood. There is an adjacent handgate, but this appears to be permanently padlocked. Descend through the wood, crossing a culverted stream at the bottom and re-ascending. Turn left with the track at the top of the rise and continue to the end of the woods. Follow the track round to the right, past a small former quarry, and arrive at a farm road.

Turn left and follow the lane past Hollyseat Farm, keeping to the right as you pass the farm buildings. Continue round a double bend and turn right at a T-junction.

Short of Hollyhouse Cottage, turn right over a stile (it may be overgrown, hidden and in poor repair), opposite a farm gate. Turn left in the field and follow the hedge past the buildings, turning left again through a farm gate. Cross the next field direct to a gate and an enclosed green lane (Shipley Lane). Follow the lane through to the road, turning left here for Shottlegate, then left again, back to the Hanging Gate.

Midshires Way – Blackbrook to Alderwasley (5 miles)

The Way follows the pub walk route along Longwalls Lane, then continues on the old road to its junction with Wilderbrook Lane. Here it turns briefly left, and then right again, forsaking the road in favour of a waymarked field path. After crossing one field, the route ascends a low ridge on a north-westerly line, still following the believed Old Portway route. As the gradient eases, Alport Hill comes into view ahead with its crown of radio aerials. The field pattern is rather confusing here, and some of the field boundaries marked on the Outdoor Leisure map are no longer in existence. So careful navigation is required, as the path swings round to north-east. The Midshires Way signs are many and frequent, but not always obvious. A new and useful waymark makes its appearance here, in the shape of the Sherwood Foresters' war memorial tower, in line ahead on Crich Cliff. The path crosses a footbridge and arrives at a road – Palerow Lane – where it turns right.

The Way continues to the end of Palerow Lane, turning right here at the T-junction to follow Belper Road for a short distance only. A footpath is then taken, via a narrow squeezer on the left (there is an interesting old milestone on the opposite verge), and follows the wall, initially in a sunken way. It then descends over the fields to Netherpark Farm, where it crosses the lane to enter Shining Cliff Woods (where there is a Youth Hostel) and join the route of Pub Walk 12, to Alderwasley Hall School.

[12] Alderwasley
Ye Olde Bear

Like the Hanging Gate, this too is an 'out of town' pub. A fine old 16th-century coaching inn, it occupies a hilltop site with splendid wide views over the Derwent valley. Alderwasley is a scattered parish, and although Ye Olde Bear is some way from the village itself, it is very much a part of the community. There are oak beams, and some bare stone walls in the several interconnecting small rooms, which include a separate, smart dining room.

This is a freehouse, offering Bass ales, Dry Blackthorn cider and lagers by Carling (Black Label) and Tennent's (Extra and Pilsner). Food is available every lunchtime, as well as on Monday to Saturday evenings, and on Sunday evenings from Easter to September. Specialities on offer include lasagne verdi, chicken curry, calamares salad, smoked salmon and king prawn provençal. There is a tempting selection of various grills, salads and snacks, as well as a range of vegetarian dishes. Families are welcome and will find a children's play area and a beer garden. Well-behaved dogs are also welcome. If you are looking for a bed, the Bear has nine en-suite rooms (including a bridal suite!). Caravan parking is also available with shower and toilet facilities.

The pub is open from 12 noon to 3 pm and 7 pm to 10.30 pm on

Sunday, 11 am to 3 pm and 6 pm to 11 pm on Monday to Friday, and all day (11 am to 11 pm) on Saturday.
Telephone: 01629 822585.

How to get there: Leave the A6 trunk road at Ambergate by Holly Lane (just south of the Hurt Arms Hotel), crossing the river Derwent and climbing steeply. Follow this road for about 2 miles to reach a crossroads. Turn right onto the Wirksworth road and continue for about ½ mile. Ye Olde Bear will be seen on your right.

Parking: There is a spacious car park for customers.

Length of the walk: 4 miles. Maps: OS Landranger 119 Buxton and Matlock, and Outdoor Leisure 24 White Peak (inn GR 314527).

This walk takes us first through pleasant woodland and over Alderwasley Park to the village itself, passing close by the Hall and church. The round is completed by a circuitous route along field paths and lanes to the Olde Bear. A welcome, if rare, discovery is that all the roads around Alderwasley appear to be prominently identified by name. A great help in describing the route!

The Walk

Leaving the pub, turn left and follow Wirksworth Road past Windmill Lane, turning left again on reaching Higg Lane. At Peat Pits (Forest Enterprise woodland), turn right, following the waymarked footpath. This is a delightful woodland walk, although possibly very wet in the lower reaches in the rainy season. There is an alternative, initially gravelled, path along the top end of the woods if the waymarked path is deemed impassable.

On meeting a broader track (T-junction) turn left, joining the Midshires Way.

Keep ahead on this new track through a field gate and continue, with the field wall and the woods on your right.

Passing through a further gate, you emerge into the spacious parkland of Alderwasley Hall, passing initially over open woodland, with birches and bracken – and excellent views ahead over the Derwent valley. A prominent feature across the valley is the long, limestone Crich Cliff, with its war memorial lighthouse.

Bear left with the track and follow it through to the road, close to Alderwasley Hall – nowadays used as a school. Bear right with the road, past the entrance to the Hall and church, continuing up the hill. Pass the end of Chapel Hill and keep on along New Road. Descend the hill (again with Crich Stand prominent a little to your right) and turn left onto the

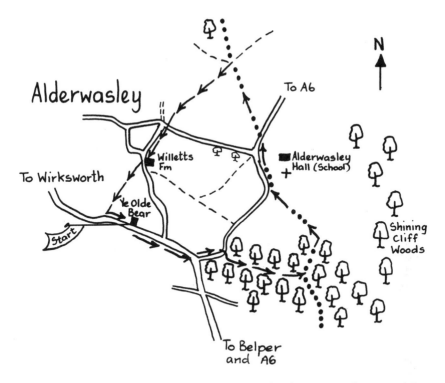

waymarked footpath. At the end of a length of green track, turn right across the end of the field, pass through a squeezer and continue left, up the field, with the hedge on your left. Continue up a second field, now on the left of the hedge. Go through another squeezer and turn left, leaving the Midshires Way.

Follow the wall to a stile and cross over, following the wall in the same direction. Bear leftward from the wall in the succeeding fields, heading for a group of farm buildings. Pass to the right of a large barn and reach the road at Bury Hill. Cross over and follow Pendleton Lane to Willetts Farm, continuing ahead up the hill, by field paths, to Wirksworth Road. Turn left, back to base.

Midshires Way – Alderwasley to Black Rocks (3½ miles)

The pub walk route is followed initially from Alderwasley Hall. Where the Midshires Way and the circular walk part company, the Way turns right instead of left, through a very tight squeezer, then left again, down the field. It bears right down the next field, and left again at the bottom, to reach Watergate Farm. Over the lane by the farm entrance, the Way climbs steeply uphill by field path to Bunting

Wood. After following a track, still uphill, the route branches right along a footpath, passing to the right of Watfield Farm. Then on through woods, descending to cross one small field and reach the Whatstandwell to Wirksworth road. The route continues along the track opposite – Intake Lane. From here to Black Rocks the route corresponds to that of Pub Walk 13 – along Intake Lane to join the High Peak Trail, ascending the steep Sheep Pasture Incline.

Alderwasley.

[13] **Wirksworth Moor**
The Malt Shovel

There is no settlement of any size at Wirksworth Moor – just a few scattered farms and occasional homesteads – but the old lead-mining town of Wirksworth is little more than a mile distant and, between these elements and the passing traffic on the local roads and footpaths, the Malt Shovel attracts a quite satisfactory volume of trade.

This is a friendly and welcoming country hostelry, clearly popular with the locals – and with the casual 'dropper-in', whether motorised or pedestrian. Pictures in the bar-room suggest that, at one time, this pub was a residential hotel, and it is noted that the present car park occupies the site of a turn-of-the-century tennis court. An interesting feature, bearing in mind the distance of Wirksworth from the coast, is a collection of naval cap-tallies!

A Marston's house, Pedigree is on offer here, and guest beers too. Strongbow cider is available on draught, wines such as du Tarn and Liebfraumilch, and both Heineken and Stella Artois lagers are provided. Meals and bar snacks are served daily from 12 noon until 2.30 pm. An impressive menu includes giant Yorkshire pudding with steak and kidney filling, chips and peas, cottage pie, lasagne, and chicken curry with rice. If you are looking for a snack, there is a varied selection of sandwiches and rolls, including the speciality Malt Shovel Special Toastie (with cheese, ham, onion, or tomato and pickle). And how about treacle sponge for afters? Families are welcome at the Malt Shovel, and accommodation includes a family room and a children's play area. Dogs are welcome inside, too – provided of course that they are well-behaved! Customers are permitted to eat their own food in the beer garden, outside catering hours.

The pub is open all day, from 12 noon to 11 pm (10.30 pm on Sunday).

Telephone: 01629 822427.

How to get there: Leave the A6 Derby to Matlock road at Whatstandwell Bridge (the Cromford end), following the B5035 steeply uphill in the direction of Wirksworth. The pub stands on the corner of the unclassified Cromford road, about 2½ miles on from here.

There is no lack of buses serving the Cromford and Wirksworth area generally, although the only service to Wirksworth Moor itself appears to be a single bus in each direction, Friday only, between Nottingham and Bonsall (Whites).

Parking: The licensee has no objection to customers leaving their vehicles in the pub car park while doing the walk. Parking facilities are also available at the Black Rocks, partway round the route.

Length of the walk: 4½ miles. Maps: OS Landranger 119 Buxton and Matlock, and Outdoor Leisure 24 White Peak (inn GR 299541).

This walk gives us our first introduction to the High Peak Trail, a long-distance route in its own right which the Midshires Way will follow for some 17 miles to Dowlow. In the course of our journey we pass the popular rock-climbing grounds at Black Rocks and continue over the pleasantly wooded and heather-clad Barrel Edge.

The Walk

Leave the pub, following the B5035 round the right-angled bend towards Whatstandwell. As you walk along this road you get a good view of the limestone face of Crich Stand, surmounted by its war memorial (Sherwood Foresters') lighthouse. Turn left at Home Farm (opposite Wigwell Grange) and follow the adjacent farm lane through to Woodstock Plantation. Cross the plantation, bearing rightward through the woods to reach and go over a stile in the far right-hand corner. Continue on a little way, turning right around the corner of the wall and walking beside it down the fields, with Crich Stand again beckoning a little to the right of your route. The wall is followed faithfully over

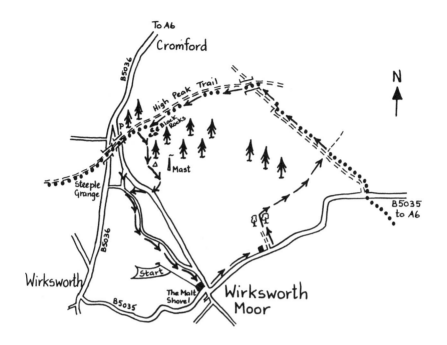

a series of fields, crossing another footpath partway along, to arrive at a rough lane, opposite a group of farm buildings, and join the Midshires Way.

Turn left along the lane (Intake Lane). After negotiating a double bend in the track, you will see, below on your right, the trackbed of the High Peak Trail ascending to meet and cross the lane by a bridge. Just before reaching the bridge, turn off left and climb up to join the Trail, turning left up the incline.

The High Peak Trail follows the trackbed of the former Cromford and High Peak Railway. Built in the first half of the 19th century (the Cromford to Hurdlow section – the present trail – was opened in 1830), the railway formed a link between the Cromford Canal and the Peak Forest Canal. The line was used mainly for the transport of freight – coal, iron, lime and other minerals, as well as agricultural goods – although a primitive passenger service was operated for a while, until a passenger died in an accident on the line. The railway had a number of extremely steep ascents, of which the Sheep Pasture Incline – where we join the Trail – is one of the most severe, ranging between 1 in 8 and 1 in 9. The engines were hauled up the gradients by steam power, operated from engine houses at the head.

Follow the incline steeply up to the Sheep Pasture Engine House,

63

where the track levels out. There are fine views here over the Cromford area, and a welcome opportunity to pause for breath.

As you reach the Black Rocks picnic site, the Midshires Way is left behind.

Bear left away from the Trail, going up past the popular Black Rocks climbing area. Keep to the extreme right and follow a clear, broad, waymarked nature-trail footpath.

At the top of the rise (by post no 5), bear right on a lesser footpath to reach a run of steps leading onto Barrel Edge, a delightful wooded rock-and-heather path with splendid wide views over the surrounding area.

Pass the triangulation pillar (noting the television mast on your left) and descend through the woods to reach and cross a stile. Bear left over one field, and right over a second, following the waymarked posts to reach a minor road.

Turn right, following the road for a short distance, leaving again by a narrow squeezer on the left. Descend, by steps and a footpath, to a residential road, The Lanes. Turn right to reach a telephone call box, then go left again into a narrow lane – Stoney Hill. Follow this through to the Wirksworth Moor road and turn right, back to the inn.

Midshires Way – Black Rocks to Middleton Top (1½ miles)

Following the Midshires Way from Black Rocks to Middleton Top – as anywhere on the High Peak Trail section – is simplicity itself, just a matter of following one's nose. After passing Steeple Grange, the Middleton Incline is reached, 708 yards at a gradient of a little more than 1 in 9. The wagons were hauled up the incline by means of a steam winding engine, which has been restored and can at certain times be seen in operation at Middleton Top.

[14] Middleton by Wirksworth
The Rising Sun

The Rising Sun occupies a prominent position on a junction of roads at Rise End, the southern extremity of Middleton, a former lead-mining village high above the Via Gellia. An inscription over the bar in the Rising Sun proclaims that 'You are a stranger here but once', an assertion confirmed by the welcoming atmosphere in this friendly and popular peakland pub. Converted from a former farmhouse, it remains a place of real character. The décor includes a proud display of sporting trophies – boules, darts and so on – and a collection of football club badges. The hospitality extends to overnight accommodation, three rooms being available, one of which (the landlord declines to reveal which) is allegedly haunted!

An Ansells house this, and the ales include Pedigree, Tetley and Kilkenny. Also on offer are Olde English Cider, Carlsberg, Castlemaine and Lowenbrau lagers, and various wines. Food is provided daily, both at lunchtime and in the evening. Specialities include steakwich in a bun, lasagne, sausage and peas, and beef curry, all served with fries and side salad. There are steak dishes, seafood, poultry and dairy ranges, plus the ubiquitous ploughman's. Filled rolls are available every day except Sunday, or you might find a tasty chip butty quite satisfying – or you can go the whole hog and enjoy a traditional Sunday lunch. Children and vegetarians are also amply catered for. Families are welcome. Dogs also, 'at certain times' – so ask.

The opening hours are from 11.30 am to 3 pm and 6 pm to 11 pm in the week and 12 noon to 3 pm and 7 pm to 10.30 pm on Sunday. Telephone: 01629 822420.

How to get there: The Rising Sun stands on the junction of the B5035 Cromford to Ashbourne and the B5023 Wirksworth to Grange Mill roads. If coming from the main A6, turn off at Cromford and follow the road steeply up past Black Rocks, turning right at the B5035 junction. The pub occupies a prominent position overlooking the next crossroads.

Trent buses from Derby, Belper, Matlock and Bakewell serve the area.

Parking: There is no objection to customers parking while they walk. Suitable provision is also available at Middleton Top, on the High Peak Trail.

Length of the walk: 3½ miles. Maps: OS Landranger 119 Buxton and Matlock, and Outdoor Leisure 24 White Peak (inn GR 279553).

You will not travel far in this part of Derbyshire without meeting the legacy of the county's industrial past. In the course of this walk we tread the trackbed of the former Cromford and High Peak Railway, and walk where 'The Owd Man' once foraged for lead. We pass quickly by a modern quarry site to stroll where spoilheaps still intrude, but where, in season, the bluebells bloom in profusion, and the views over the Peakland hills are glorious.

The Walk

Cross the road to the left of the pub and follow the minor road opposite, uphill and under the bridge. Immediately after the bridge go left up the footpath to join the High Peak Trail and turn left. Cross the bridge now, and continue steeply up the Middleton Incline to reach Middleton Top. Middleton Top is one of the high points – in more ways than one – of the High Peak Trail. The winding engine, the only one of the original eight still surviving, has been restored and, at certain times, the impressive engine house is open to visitors. There is a visitor centre here too. And bicycles for hire. Before continuing, you are recommended to visit the viewfinder in the car park, and try to pick out a few of the features, far and near, to be seen from this viewpoint.

Continue on along the trail, enjoying the wide views over to the left. Prominent on the skyline is the conglomeration of aerials pin-pointing

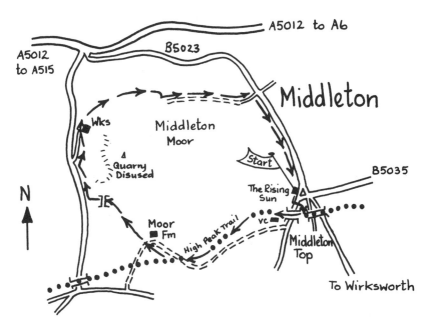

the location of Alport Hill, a few miles away on the other side of
Wirksworth. There is a good, hard surface here for walking, but the
steep sides of the cuttings have reverted well to nature, with wild flowers
in great profusion in the summer months.

At a junction with a crossing track, leave the High Peak Trail, and the
Midshires Way.

Bear right, following the track past a group of farm buildings. As the
track bends leftward after the farm, keep straight ahead over a stile,
following the waymarked footpath on the left of the wall. Keep to the
right of the fields, straying leftward at one point to cross the wall, before
returning to the original wallside line. Cross to the right of the wall now,
and continue under a derelict mineral line to reach Armlees Farm and
the road.

Turn right and follow the road till you reach a works entrance. Bear
right up the service road and through the barrier. Keep to the left of the
buildings, bearing left at the far end to join a green track to the left of a
quarry area.

Follow the track and succeeding footpath up through woodland
onto Middleton Moor. This has all the appearances of derelict land,
a prominent feature being the spoilheaps from ancient mine workings.
But do not be misled. It is a delightful walk along a little-used path, with
glorious views over the Griffe Grange valley and the Via Gellia road, to

the north. The Via Gellia is a scenic road and the name is a play on words. It means 'way of lilies', and it was planted many years ago with lilies of the valley by a local industrialist called Gell – so the name could also be translated as Gell's Way! Sadly, there are no lilies today. But there are plenty of ramsons (wild garlic) to perfume the air in early summer! And wild flowers are everywhere in season, with prolific bluebells in spring, as well as cowslips, primroses and red campion – not to mention the rare pyramidal orchis. But keep to the path. This is old lead land, and open shafts are not unknown in this part of the world.

The path gravitates to a stile on the edge of the moor, leading into a green lane. Follow the track to its junction with a farm lane and turn left. This is a fine, high track, with the gaunt mass of Riber Castle prominent on the skyline above Matlock. As you proceed towards Middleton, you will also see the long escarpment of Crich Cliff topped by its war memorial lighthouse.

Follow the road down to join the B5023 road in Middleton, opposite the Nelson Arms inn. Turn right and continue back to the Rising Sun.

Midshires Way – Middleton Top to Longcliffe (4 miles)

The Way follows the route described in the pub walk for the first ½ mile, after which it continues on along the High Peak Trail all the way to Longcliffe – and beyond. This is another easy stretch, with wide views and easy walking. After passing through the gloom of Hopton Tunnel, the route ascends the Hopton Incline, the site of a fatal derailment in 1937. Points of interest to look out for along the way include Carsington Reservoir and Harborough Rocks.

[15] Brassington
The Miners Arms

Brassington is a typical hill village close to the line of The Street – the Roman road from Derby to Buxton – and much of the village, which includes many buildings dating from the 16th to 18th centuries, is in a designated conservation area.

The Miners Arms is a fine old, traditional village pub, with a centrally situated open fireplace and a cosy lounge/dining area. The building dates back to the early 17th century and the first mention of a pub here was in the manorial rolls of 1747. The miners in the title were lead miners, and the name is appropriate, because the local Barmote or court used to meet here to adjudicate miners' claims.

A Marston's house, the ales include Bitter, Pedigree and Head Brewer's Choice and Batemans Mild. The cider is Strongbow, and lagers are by Carlsberg and Kronenbourg. Food is available every lunchtime from 12 noon to 2 pm and in the evenings, except Wednesday, from 7 pm to 9 pm. There is a traditional Sunday lunch, subject to advance booking. All the food is home-prepared, with an impressive range of main dishes – sirloin steak, mussels in garlic, white wine and cream, beef, mushroom and Guinness pie, vegetarian sausage and onion yorkie – to name but a few. The tempting selection of afters includes such old favourites as bread and butter pudding, spotted dick, treacle sponge and fruit crumble. If you only require a snack, you can choose from a variety of filled rolls. Families are welcome: dogs, too, if well-behaved. And bed and breakfast accommodation can be provided.

The lunchtime hours are from 12 noon to 2.30 pm on Monday to Friday, and to 3 pm on Saturday and Sunday. Evening opening is from 6.30 pm to 11 pm on Monday to Saturday and 7 pm to 10.30 pm on Sunday.

Telephone: 01629 540222.

How to get there: From the A5012 Cromford to Newhaven (Via Gellia) road, turn south-west at Grange Mill, following the B5056 Ashbourne road for about 2 miles, to the Longcliffe crossroads. Turn left, passing under the High Peak Trail, and continue ahead to Brassington. The Miners Arms is in the centre of the village, almost opposite the parish church.

Buses between Ashbourne, Wirksworth and Matlock (Express Motors) stop at Brassington church.

Parking: You may leave your car here while you walk. The only alternative facilities consist of limited on-street parking.

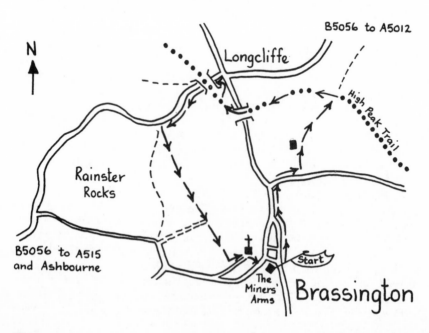

Length of the walk: 3½ miles. Maps: OS Landranger 119 Buxton and Matlock, and Outdoor Leisure 24 White Peak (inn GR 231543).

Brassington is one of many Derbyshire villages whose economy, in the past, was largely based on lead mining. The mining has died out today, although evidence of it is everywhere. Much of the ground here is rocky, and marked with the signs of ancient workings, now grassed over. We also follow the Midshires Way along a further section of the High Peak Trail.

The Walk

Cross the road in front of the pub, following the road opposite to its junction with the Longcliffe to Carsington road, and turn left, climbing steadily. At a junction (signposted for Wirksworth and Cromford) turn right, still climbing.

Leave the road at the entrance to Roundlow Farm, turning left to follow the waymarked footpath along the farm road. Reaching the farm, pass between the farmhouse and a barn on its left, and go through the gate into the field. Cross the field, following a cart track and keeping the wall on your right until near the top of the rise. Bear right then, making for a group of trees in the corner of the field.

Through the squeezer to the left of a metal field gate, follow the wall on your right over two fields, and go through a narrow piece of woodland, to join the High Peak Trail – and the Midshires Way.

The Trail is followed, leftwards, for about a mile, passing first through a pleasantly wooded cutting, and continuing over the Brassington road and round a right-hand turn, to reach the site of the former Longcliffe station, where ends, on this occasion, our brief acquaintance with the Midshires Way.

Descend to the road and turn left, passing under the bridge. Follow the B5056 road round a double bend, passing a wood on your left and enjoying the magnificent wide views. Turn left at a waymarked bridleway close to a rocky hillock. A little way along, turn left again through a gateway, just before a barn, following the wall round the building to reach a squeezer. Through here, continue ahead for the short distance to the end of the lane, then bear left up the slope to a second squeezer in the far corner of the field.

Keep to a similar line in the next field, passing through a gateway (no gate) and continuing along a faint path over 'troubled ground'. This is a former mining area, with lots of humps and holes, but no evidence from the footpath of any old shafts. But take care, and stick to the path.

After two such fields, a lane-end is crossed, the path then continuing over the hill. The distant view here includes a glimpse of Carsington Reservoir. Descend to join a lane on the outskirts of Brassington and turn left till you see the church, in the dip on your right. Follow the footpath steeply down by the side of the graveyard, turning left at the bottom to reach the pub.

Midshires Way – Longcliffe to Hurdlow (10 miles)
This is one of the longer sections of the Midshires Way, basically because there is a dearth of watering holes between Longcliffe and Hurdlow. The Way still follows the High Peak Trail all the way. You are unlikely to see any Midshires Way double-acorn waymarks along the way, but that is no problem. It would take a very determined failure to lose his way on this long, thin ribbon of track. Notable landmarks are the prominent tree-capped Minninglow Hill – a Bronze Age burial site – the Friden Brick Works and Parsley Hay 'station', a good place for light refreshments.

[16] Hurdlow
The Bull i' th' Thorn

Hurdlow Town – really no more than a couple of farms – sits at the foot of Cronkston Low, about half a mile from the site of Hurdlow station, the northernmost parking area on the High Peak Trail, and just off the main Ashbourne to Buxton road. Dating back over 500 years, the Bull, a former coaching inn, has tremendous character. There are ancient stone-flagged floors and panelled walls, and the big open fireplace and heavy old beams proclaim the hostelry's foundation date of 1472. The furnishings include a very old refectory-style table, and carved settles and chairs, with a miscellany of period militaria – swords, cutlasses, pistols and armoury – occupying the walls. Originally known as the Bull from early on and then as the Hurdlow House, it later reverted to the Bull. When the district became briefly, Hurdlow Thorn, this was adapted for the pub in local dialect as the Bull i' th' Thorn.

This is a Robinson's house and their Best Bitter is among the ales. The cider is Strongbow, and Carling Black Label and Einhorn lagers are on offer. There is a full wine list, but the speciality of the house is Allouette. Food is served both at lunchtime and in the evenings and includes a varied selection of sandwiches and salads. If you require something more substantial, you could choose from a full range of main dishes, such as steak and kidney pie, roast beef, sirloin steak or chicken in a basket. Baked potatoes are usually available, either as an alternative to chips, or on their own with a variety of tasty fillings. There is a choice of sweets to complete the meal. Rambling parties can be catered for here, by prior arrangement. Families are welcome, and there is both a family room and a children's play area, as well as a beer garden. Dogs, if well-behaved, are welcome too. The Bull also provides bed and breakfast accommodation, in addition to a holiday flat and facilities for camping and caravanning.

On Monday to Saturday the pub is open from 11 am to 3 pm – with some flexibility – and 6.30 pm to 11 pm. Sunday hours are from 12 noon to 3 pm and 7 pm to 10.30 pm.

Telephone: 01298 83348.

How to get there: The Bull is a prominent, half-timbered building on the eastern side of the A515 Ashbourne to Buxton road, about 6 miles south of Buxton.

Parking: You are welcome to make use of the pub car park. An alternative recommendation (which can cut ½ mile from your walking distance) is to drive over to, and park at, the Hurdlow car park on the High Peak Trail.

Length of the walk: 4 miles. Maps: OS Landranger 119 Buxton and Matlock and Outdoor Leisure 24 White Peak (inn GR 128665).

On this walk we take our leave, for the last time, of the High Peak Trail, which has been our host for the past 17 miles of the Midshires Way. We return to the starting point along quiet lanes and unfrequented paths and byways – with a possible opportunity for further refreshment at the former railway station inn.

The Walk
From the Bull, cross the road, taking extreme care. This is a long, straight stretch of fast main road. Through the farm gate directly opposite the inn, cross the field and follow the guide-posts to reach the High Peak Trail, accessed by a footpath on the left, nearside, of a bridge.

On the Trail, turn right and follow it for 1½ miles. Here, at Dowlow, the High Peak Trail ends and we leave it and the Midshires Way, turning left along a grassy lane.

Follow the lane south, crossing a long-abandoned railway track (no public access). At the top of the hill pause for a few moments to admire the splendid views ahead over the myriad hills around the Dove and Manifold valleys.

Go on a little way and turn left through a squeezer, following the left

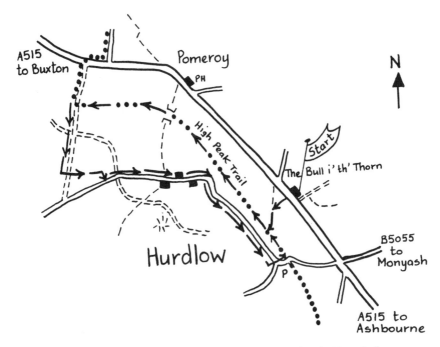

of the wall over flower-rich, traditional pasture-land. You feel you are on top of the world here, at well over 1,000 ft above sea level, with magnificent views in every direction.

Cross a stile, by a guide-post, and cross straight over the next field to reach a minor road and turn left. Pass again the same abandoned railway. There is evidence of some access here, but this is a red-herring, as the track is over private land, and does not appear to lead anywhere useful. The hill behind (Cronkston Low) is of some interest however, as there is a tumulus on its summit and evidence which suggests a hill fort site.

Follow the quiet minor road through the tiny settlement of Hurdlow Town and on to Hurdlow car park, on the site of the former Cromford and High Peak Railway station. The Royal Oak Inn here is a useful refreshment point at certain times. Otherwise, the return route to the Bull is via the trail for a little way, then back over the fields, following the outward route in reverse.

Midshires Way – Hurdlow to Chelmorton (4½ miles)

The Way follows the pub walk route to the end of the High Peak Trail, where it turns right, to reach the main (A515) road. Here it turns right again, and left at the next turning. After passing Blinder House, the road bends left, but the Midshires Way continues straight ahead, now following a green lane over the high limestone plateau of central Derbyshire. There are extensive views to the east and – later – to the west.

At the end of the lane, the Way turns left. A road sign at the next turning points ahead for Chelmorton, but the Midshires Way route turns right here to reach the top end of the village, close to the church and the pub.

The High Peak Trail, Hurdlow.

[17] Chelmorton
The Church Inn

The ancient settlement of Chelmorton is somewhat unusual – one of the few surviving examples of a traditional Peakland medieval village which still retains the ancient pattern of long, narrow fields, enclosed within a network of green lanes. It is happily situated astride a quiet byroad, and the first view seen by the rambler approaching over the fields from Taddington is the tall church spire, topped by its unusual grasshopper weathervane.

As you might expect, the Church Inn is situated directly opposite the church, and is a deservedly popular watering-hole for the many hungry hikers, weary walkers and tired travellers who pass this way. A typical stone-built Derbyshire property, parts of the building are said to date back to the 12th century. It is a freehouse and some of the ales on offer are Marston's Pedigree and Bitter, Adnams Southwold Bitter and Bateman Dark Mild. You can choose either Strongbow or Woodpecker cider, or lagers by Foster's and Heineken. Liebfraumilch and Soave are among the featured wines. Food is available daily and an appetizing selection of bar snacks includes fried scampi with tartare sauce, gammon steak with pineapple, lasagne verdi and fried chicken with bacon. Or how about a chip butty with salad garni? There are also daily specials – such as

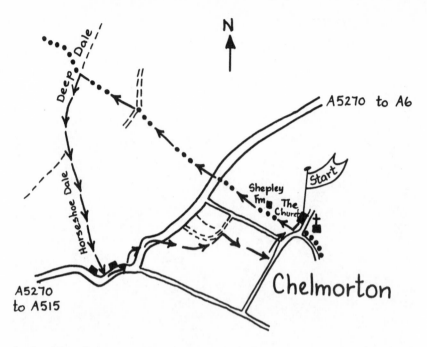

fresh plaice fillet, or topside of beef – advertised on the bar blackboard. Families are welcome, as also are well-behaved dogs. There is no beer garden as such but you will find an outside eating/drinking area. Bed and breakfast accommodation is available too.

The pub is open in the week from 11 am to 3 pm and 7 pm to 11 pm, and on Sunday from 12 noon to 3 pm and 7 pm to 10.30 pm.

Telephone: 01298 85319.

How to get there: From the A6 Buxton to Bakewell or the A515 Buxton to Ashbourne road, follow the A5270 Calton to Brierlow link road. Turn off east on the bend 1 mile east of Brierlow Bar, then take the next turn left to arrive in Chelmorton. The Church Inn is on the left at the top of the main street.

Chelmorton is served by a Buxton to Monyash circular bus route (Bowers) – not on Sunday.

Parking: The pub has no car park, but there is ample roadside space in the vicinity.

Length of the walk: 4 miles. Maps: OS Landranger 119 Buxton and Matlock, and Outdoor Leisure 24 (White Peak) (inn GR 115703).

Chelmorton lies at around 1,200 ft, high on the limestone plateau of the White Peak. The village is dominated to the north by Chelmorton Low, but our walk is mostly over easy gradients, on field paths, green lanes and dry dales. You will find just one tricky hillside descent to test your mettle.

The Walk

Walk down the hill from the pub, turning right opposite Church Lane. Follow the stony lane – waymarked to 'Old Coalpit Lane'. Stay with this, passing Shepley Farm, to reach the A5270 road (the Old Coalpit Lane referred to). Ignore the walled lane directly opposite, crossing the road half-left to join another stone road. This is a fine, high way, and provides easy walking on a gently declining track, where you stride out purposefully, making the most of the glorious views and enjoying, perhaps, the song of a lark or the call of a curlew.

Where the road curves right, turn off left onto a green lane, leaving this almost immediately via a squeezer on the right. Cross four fields on a diagonal line to reach a stile leading out onto the lip of Deep Dale.

Descend with care to the floor of the dale. The path is steep and narrow, and extreme delicacy of footwork is demanded, particularly if conditions are damp – wet limestone and rubber soles are not the ideal partnership! Near the bottom of the path a small but deep cave invites exploration.

Turn left at the foot of the path, ignoring the one opposite, which conducts the Midshires Way on towards Buxton.

Our path climbs easily up through the wooded dale, ascending first to pass another, larger, cave, before continuing over alternating surfaces of loose scree and rocky footpath.

At the head of Deep Dale, a stile leads out into the more open, grassy Horseshoe Dale, joining the ancient Priest's Way path. After the climb down into, and the rough track through, Deep Dale, it is a distinct joy to walk on the short green sward of Horseshoe Dale. After about ½ mile, pass a small side valley (Bullhay Dale), bearing right with the farm track to pass the Dale Grange Farm buildings and reach the A5270 road.

Turn left along the road, passing Dale Grange farmhouse, and continue around a couple of bends, using the broad verges where practicable. Leave again by the first green lane on the right. At the end of the lane, bear left a little over the field to reach a stile beside a gate. Turn right into another green lane, and left again with the track, looking out for a stile on the right – which you will find, again beside a field gate, leading into the third field along.

Follow the wall on your right, then that on your left down a second field. Pass close by a cottage (up the garden path!) and follow the concrete farm road to Main Street. Turn left, back to the Church Inn.

Midshires Way – Chelmorton to Bunsal Cob (10½ miles)

The Way follows the pub walk route as far as Deep Dale. The delicate descent into the dale is followed by a slightly easier ascent on the far side, after which the Way follows the wall over the fields to reach the road by King Sterndale church. Turning left here, the route leaves the road again, on the right, crossing over broad parkland pastures to Cowdale, then continues on the same general line to Staden, from where it descends, passing a caravan site and beneath a viaduct to reach the road at Harpur Hill (by the Youth Hostel) on the outskirts of Buxton.

The main road is followed through Buxton, passing the Market Place and continuing ahead to leave by the A5004, Whaley Bridge road. About 2 miles out of the town the road bends left, but the Midshires Way keeps straight ahead on the line of the old Roman road – a minor road – which is followed as far as the White Hall Outdoor Pursuits Centre. From here, the Way follows the route described in Pub Walk 18, as far as Bunsal Cob car park.

[18] Fernilee
The Shady Oak

The Shady Oak stands alongside the Buxton road (Long Hill), in the hamlet of Fernilee, south of Whaley Bridge. Despite the small size of the settlement, Fernilee district covers a considerable area which includes the Fernilee Reservoir, down below in the Goyt Valley. This historic inn offers a warm welcome, and an appetizing and wholesome table to walkers, cyclists and motorists – indeed, to all comers. The house belongs to the Real Inns group and the ales served include Boddingtons Bitter and Dark Mild. Lagers are Heineken, Stella and Labatts, the cider is Strongbow, and there is a choice of wines, red, white and rosé. Food is available both at lunchtime and in the evening, until 2.15 pm and 9.30 pm. You may pick from a comprehensive range of starters, grills, home-made pies and quiches, roasts, fish dishes and sweets. If you fancy a quick snack, you could try the Shady Shepherd's Pie or a delicious sandwich or salad. There is a special children's menu, and tea and coffee are also available. Families are welcome; and so are well-behaved dogs. There are picnic tables on the front, and the landlord does not mind genuine customers (ie, those buying drinks) eating their own sandwiches there – but he does object to non-customers using the frontage as a public picnic site!

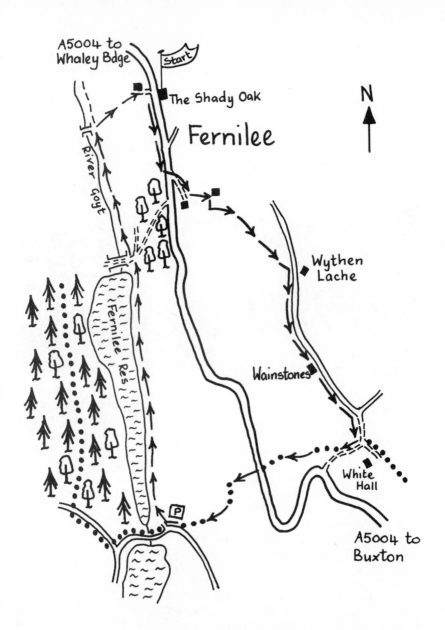

A5004 to Whaley Bdge

Start

The Shady Oak

Fernilee

River Goyt

N

Wythen Lache

Fernilee Res

Wainstones

White Hall

P

A5004 to Buxton

Lunchtime opening is from 11.30 am to 3 pm in the week and 12 noon to 3 pm on Sunday. Evening times are from 7 pm to 11 pm on Monday and Tuesday, 6 pm to 11 pm on Wednesday to Saturday, and 7 pm to 10.30 pm on Sunday.
Telephone: 01663 732212.

How to get there: Follow the Long Hill road (A5004) south from Whaley Bridge or north from Buxton. The Shady Oak is a prominent building on the eastern side of the road in the hamlet of Fernilee, about 2 miles south of Whaley Bridge.
There are buses between Whaley Bridge and Fernilee (Bowers), but not on Sunday.

Parking: There is no objection to customers parking here while they walk. An excellent alternative is the Bunsal Cob car park, partway round the route, by Errwood Reservoir.

Length of the walk: 5½ miles. Maps: OS Landranger 119 Buxton and Matlock, and Outdoor Leisure 24 (White Peak) (inn GR 016790).

The Goyt valley is one of the most wildly beautiful areas of the Peak District. The winding Long Hill road follows its sinuous course high above the scenic beauties of Fernilee and Errwood Reservoirs. In the course of our walk, we follow a long down-graded Roman road, and walk the abandoned track of the Cromford and High Peak Railway.

The Walk
Follow the main road towards Buxton, crossing the end of Elnor Lane. After going over a stream, bear left onto a farm lane. A little way up the lane cross a stile on the left and follow the fence up the field, bearing left to reach and cross a stile leading to Overhill Farm.
Turn right along the farm lane, through the gateway, and then left as indicated by the arrow waymark. Follow the track over two fields. Turn half-right in the third field, steering to the left of a dip in the distant ridge and making for the farm buildings at Wythen Lache. Reaching a boggy area towards the top of the field, follow the stream to the right to find the best way over, continuing then to cross a stile and reach the road.
Turn right along the road, climbing up through the cutting by Wainstones Farm. Following this narrow and peaceful hill road today it is hard to realise that you are on a Roman road, and that this was once the main route between Buxton and Manchester, until it was replaced by John Metcalf's Long Hill road. Metcalf was a renowned road builder and was responsible for a number of significant improvements to routes around Buxton in particular and elsewhere in the Peak District.

The Midshires Way is joined at the entrance to the White Hall Outdoor Pursuits Centre. Turn right here onto a secondary farm track. At a field gate, turn right again, over a stile this time, following the wall as directed. Beyond the next stile bear left along a very clear track, passing around the angle of a wall and continuing over and down the hillside to meet the A5004 road. As you cross the fields from White Hall, you will see below on your left the modern winding road. The present road loops round here to avoid a steep descent in Metcalf's original road, but the old section can still be seen, in the form of a green lane connecting the two ends of the loop road.

Cross the road and continue ahead. Leave the farm track at the second bend, following the footpath straight in front, waymarked for Bunsal Cob and Errwood Dam. Cross a footbridge and continue through to the road at Bunsal Cob car park.

Leaving the Midshires Way, follow the fence down to the Fernilee Reservoir access road and the reservoir-side track. This is another section of the old Cromford and High Peak Railway, but it went out of use many years before the more southerly section, due to the opening of the Ashbourne to Buxton line.

Continue on the track as far as the Fernilee Dam and cross the road, following the fence down to join the waterworks access road. Beyond the buildings, go along a rough track and over a couple of fields beside the river Goyt.

Pass a footbridge and turn right at a 'Peak and Northern Counties' footpath sign. There is little evidence of a path on the ground, but another footbridge should be visible ahead. Cross, and continue up the field, keeping to the left of the stream and bearing left over marshy ground to reach a stile. Cross the next field direct, making for the farm/stable buildings. Go over a stile into the farm road and follow this down to the main road, opposite the Shady Oak.

Midshires Way – Bunsal Cob to Furness Vale (8 miles)

From the car park, the route crosses the Errwood Dam, turning right at the road junction and continuing up the hill. Where the road bends left, entering the forest, the Way continues ahead, following the forestry road high above Fernilee Reservoir. The reservoir itself is hidden from view by the curvature of the ground, but until the forest closes in there is a good view across the valley to the Long Hill road and Combs Edge. The woodland contains a pleasing mixture of mature broadleaves interspersed with stands of various conifers.

Above the Fernilee Dam, the Way leaves the trees, continuing ahead past Oldfield Farm and on along a field track beside a conifer plantation. After passing Normanwood Farm a green lane leads round to the right, continuing as a field track, and providing superb views of hills and woodland – with the Shady Oak visible on the road below.

Passing through a farm gate, just before a cottage, the Way doubles back left to follow a lane to Madscar Farm. It continues along the lane on the left of the farm, doubling around the bend and continuing up the hill to Overton Hall Farm. Here it turns right, following the lane through to Taxal village.

Immediately after the church, the Way enters a field on the right, following a footpath parallel with the road, continuing through woodland and passing the entrance to Taxal Lodge School. It now bears right, following the perimeter of a field to reach the Kettleshulme road. Crossing the road, the route continues along Reddish Lane, bearing right at the end to pass the Toddbrook Dam and descend to the river Goyt, and on into Whaley Bridge.

The Goyt Way is joined at the canal basin, from where the towpath is followed, crossing the Buxworth Arm, as far as bridge no 31, at Furness Vale.

Whaley Bridge.

[19] Furness Vale
The Soldier Dick

To the traveller passing through, the industrial village of Furness Vale can make no claims to prettiness – but appearances can be deceptive. Leave the main road and, within minutes, you will find yourself in the idyllic surroundings of the Peak Forest Canal, with the Furness Vale Marina full of beautiful, brightly-painted narrow boats.

The name of this 17th-century inn on the main road recalls the curious tale of a stranger who arrived nearly four centuries ago, wounded and feverish, at the door of a village hostelry. Little was known of him, except that his name was Richard and he was, or had been, a soldier. He was given food and shelter, and a home at the inn, where he became a familiar and popular figure, particularly skilled with horses. We are told that, at that time, the inn was situated some way higher up on the moor, and that Dick himself actually helped in the building of the house that now bears his name, on the busier highway.

This is a freehouse, and the range of ales includes Theakston, Boddingtons, Stones and Bass. There is Tennent's Extra and Carling lager, and Strongbow and Olde English cider. Food is available daily, both at lunchtime and in the evening. There is a full range of starters and main courses to choose from, with dishes ranging from such tempters as escalope of Scottish salmon, T-bone steak, or home-made steak pie, down to the humbler sausage or beefburger, served with chips and peas. Quick snacks include cheese or ham toasties, burgers and traditional sandwiches. There is a special children's menu, and vegetarians are also catered for. Families are welcome here and there is a family room. Well-behaved dogs are welcome too.

The pub is open all day, every day. Overnight accommodation is also available.

Telephone: 01663 743868.

How to get there: Furness Vale is a linear settlement on the main A6 trunk road, between New Mills and Whaley Bridge. The Soldier Dick is on the west side of the road, in the village centre.

The pub is not far from a railway station, with a frequent daily service between Manchester, Stockport and Buxton. Various buses serve Furness Vale too, from Macclesfield, New Mills, Stockport, Buxton, Nottingham and Derby.

Parking: Patrons are welcome to park here while they walk.

Length of the walk: 4 miles. Maps: OS Landranger 110 Sheffield and Huddersfield, and Outdoor Leisure 1 Dark Peak (inn GR 006836).

Our route first follows the towpath of the Peak Forest Canal, past a splendid array of narrow boats, before taking us up onto the lower slopes of Chinley Churn, with wide views over moorland and valley.

The Walk
Cross the road and turn right, continuing to the junction with Station Road. Turn left here and go over the railway and canal bridges, turning left again then to join the towpath – and the Midshires Way.

Follow the towpath, with the canal and marina on your left, admiring the narrow boats as you go. This is the Peak Forest Canal, forming a part of both the Goyt Way and the Midshires Way. That the Way should follow the canal is a natural progression because – a point not to be overlooked – the Cromford and High Peak Railway, the route of which we followed along the High Peak Trail and, later, beside Fernilee Reservoir, was constructed to link this same waterway with the Cromford Canal.

The marina ends at a little swing bridge, and the towpath continues along a quieter stretch of water. Passing beneath a more substantial footbridge, turn sharp right to double back, parallel at first with the towpath, along a clear, well-trodden footpath, and continue down to the river Goyt. Cross the footbridge here and continue, turning left by Goytside Farm.

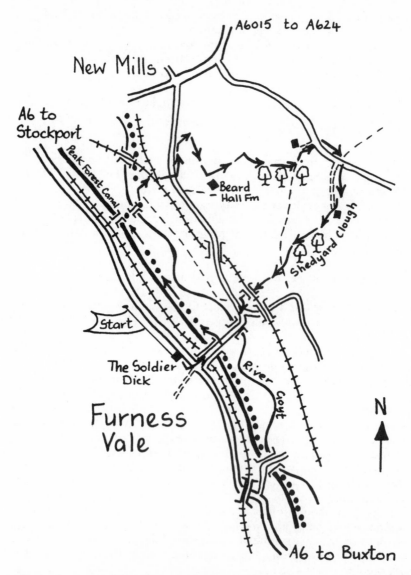

Leave the Midshires Way, turning right to follow an enclosed footpath up the hillside. Pass under the railway and continue, turning left at a road.

Follow the road to the top of the rise, then turn right up a run of steps beside garages. Follow a narrow path up the hillside to reach a concrete roadway by a row of bungalows. Turn right up the hillside here, hugging the wallside, to arrive at a farm track.

Turn right, ignoring the footpath before you, and follow the farm track up to Beard Hall Farm. Pass the bungalow by the entrance, turning left immediately through a squeezer, passing around the left side of the farm and following the wall on your left up the field.

At the end of the second field, pass through the gateway and turn right, following the green path as indicated by a white-painted arrow, with a wooded slope declining on your right. Continue over several challenging stiles, to turn left into an enclosed footpath, with a wooded hill on your right. Turn right by Ballbeard Farm, and right again at a T-junction (Laneside Road).

Follow Laneside Road towards the moor, turning right after about ¹/₂ mile onto the Shedyard Farm lane, a quiet country lane, making for pleasant, easy walking. At the farm, bear right to a gate in the far right-hand corner, hidden as you approach around the corner of a small building. Pass through the gate and continue along a little-used grassy way above the wooded dell of Shedyard Clough.

Continue over a large field and descend by rough, moorish ground to join a farm track. Turn left over the stream, leaving the track again at a guide-post on the right. The stile here is another challenger – and you may well find the gate easier. Descend over the field direct to a bridge under the railway, and pass through. Follow the wall past an electricity pylon to descend by a run of steps to the road. Turn right, then left, back to Station Road and Furness Vale.

Midshires Way – Furness Vale to Brook Bottom (4 miles)

The pub walk route is followed as far as Goytside Farm, where the Way turns left to follow the farm lane under the viaduct and enter the Torrs Riverside Park, a fascinating 'Park under the Town' of New Mills, where the rivers Sett and Goyt unite beneath mighty bridges and viaducts. The waymarked path ascends to the Rock Tavern, continuing via Torvale Road and passing close to the Torvale Mill, then through woodland to meet a minor road.

The road is left again by a track on the left, between a pair of houses, leading onto a riverside footpath. After passing through a bridlegate, the path bears right up the wooded bank to reach the Hague Bar car park. Here the route turns right along Waterside Road, crossing the railway and the New Mills to Marple road and continuing steeply up the minor road ahead. After passing the Hague Fold farms this reverts to a rough track, still climbing, to meet the Brook Bottom Road. Here it turns left, to reach the Fox Inn.

[20] Brook Bottom
The Fox Inn

As the first of our selection of pubs stood on the very edge of Leicestershire, so the last one sits right on the Derbyshire/Cheshire border. Indeed, the hamlet of Brook Bottom straddles the county boundary, with one foot in each camp, a mile outside the town of New Mills, at the end of a narrow cul-de-sac – literally buried in the hills.

The Fox is a snug little pub, with a most obliging licensee. The walls are decorated with, among other memorabilia, a series of old song-sheets. There is an impressive range of brassware on the mantelshelf, ironware in the hearth, and implements (saws, sickles and so on) on the chimney breast. This is a Robinson's house, with Best Bitter, Frederic's Premium, Hatters Mild and Guinness all on draught, Strongbow cider and both Tennent's and Carlsberg lager. Food is available every lunchtime and in the evening until about 9.30 pm. An impressive range of snacks includes jacket potatoes, chilli con carne with rice, lasagne verdi, fisherman's pie, moussaka and chicken curry, all served with a salad garnish, roll and butter. If you fancy a full meal, there is a choice of starters and main courses, including steaks, chicken, scampi, deep-fried plaice, beef and kidney pie or cheese and tomato pizza, with a tempting selection of delicious sweets to follow. Families are welcome and will find a special children's menu. There is a beer garden, and dogs are welcome, if on a lead.

Sunday opening is from 12 noon to 3 pm and 7 pm to 10.30 pm. Weekday times are rather more extended, generally from 11.30 am to 3 pm and 5.30 pm to 11 pm, but winter evening sessions begin an hour later. The pub is sometimes open all day on summer Saturdays. Telephone: 01614 271634.

How to get there: From New Mills town centre (the B6101 road), follow St Mary's Road and High Lea Road – both signposted for Brook Bottom – and continue through to the end of the road, the Fox Inn.

There is no bus service nearer than New Mills. But there is a regular rail service, seven days a week, between New Mills and Manchester, which calls at Strines, $^1/_2$ mile away (request stop).

Parking: The licensee has no objection in principle to patrons leaving their vehicles here while they walk, but ask first. It has been known for visitors' cars to obstruct someone's exit or turning space.

Length of the walk: $4^1/_2$ miles. Maps: OS Landranger 109 Manchester, and Pathfinder 741 Stockport South (inn GR 986864).

Although the pub is in Derbyshire (just!), most of the walk is in Cheshire – or perhaps, to be precise, within the Metropolitan Borough of Stockport. Most of the way, too, is easy walking on good farm roads and ancient tracks. There is just one really steep section, and that can be avoided (at the expense of a superlative viewpoint).

The Walk

Follow the Goyt Way guide-post down a broad track, with a deep, wooded glen on your right. Pass under the bridge at Strines station and continue down the road a little way, turning right at a bridleway sign by a large house (Brookwood).

Follow the lane over the railway, passing a collection of farm buildings, and turn left at the next guide-post. At a junction of paths, keep to the right and remain with the clear track alongside the railway. Pass Richmond Farm and go under the railway once more, still following the same track and joining the river Goyt.

Pass Strawberry Hill (the name of a house), noting an attractive footbridge below on the left. Ignore a side path just beyond here and continue, passing what looks like a former toll house, and go under a viaduct to reach the Roman Lakes.

The lakes (it isn't clear whether they are really Roman) are a popular recreational area, and you are likely to see quite a few anglers here.

Rowing boats are available for hire, and – more important for the weary traveller – refreshments.

Follow Lakes Road to the next junction and turn right over the brook, leaving the Midshires Way.

At a 'Peak and Northern' footpath sign, branch right to follow the Cobden Edge path, passing Old Hall Farm and climbing steeply up a stony, wooded track. At the right time of the year you can enjoy the heady scent of wild garlic. A paved footway alongside parts of the track also adds to the pleasure.

Past the entrance to Linnet Clough Scout Camp, continue ahead on a metalled roadway and go round the bend, with a golf clubhouse on the left. At the next bend turn sharp right onto a more level, but poorer surfaced, road, with the golf course on either side. Follow this road as far as The Banks.

By keeping straight on here, you will eventually arrive back at Brook Bottom. But you are strongly recommended to ignore that temptation, which would deprive you of the opportunity to enjoy a superb view.

Turn left past The Banks, climbing a steep hollow way. This is the most strenuous part of the walk, so take your time – it is well worth the effort.

Emerging onto a minor road, keep straight on, making for a prominent cross on the hilltop. At the junction, bear right up the steep path ahead to reach the immense wooden cross, on the edge of a disused quarry. There is nothing to indicate the significance of the cross, but it is most probably intended as a form of Calvary. Suffice it to say that this is a significant landmark over a considerable area and, at around 1,000 ft, a superb viewpoint. You can see distant hills (North Wales?) as well as the vast panorama of Stockport and Manchester – as with any great conurbation, their attraction enhanced by distance!

Descend to the roadway and turn left, passing a white house and continuing ahead on a rough moorland track. Turn right at a guide-post to follow an enclosed green lane, with lovely views of the rolling hills of the Derbyshire/Cheshire border.

At Higher Capstone Farm turn left and walk on the access road as far as the next bend. Join a field path here and follow the wall down, descending past a small disused quarry and passing to the left of a poultry house. In the next field turn right and follow the wall to a lane, where you turn left, back to Brook Bottom.

Midshires Way – Brook Bottom to Stockport (12 miles)

The Way follows the pub walk route as far as the Roman Lakes, continuing on along the road, and turning left at the T-junction to arrive at Bottoms Bridge. The road is left here by a footpath on the left, leading steeply up through the woods to cross the railway and a road and rejoin the Peak Forest Canal towpath. After passing the visitors' moorings, a bridge is crossed at the junction with the Macclesfield Canal, and the Way descends beside a series of 16 locks.

After the penultimate lock (numbered 2), the canal is left again, as a footpath descends to join and follow the river Goyt upstream. On reaching a pony exercise area, turn left and cross the Iron (foot) Bridge, continuing ahead along the ensuing lane to Compstall. Turn left here for the Etherow Country Park (refreshments and toilets), and the end of the Goyt Way.

The Midshires Way continues on the route of the Valley Way, returning along the road to join the riverside path (river Etherow) on the nearside, right, of the road bridge. The route leads through woodland, bearing right at the end to pass Lower and Upper Watermeetings farms, then on up the hill to a stile on the left, close by a tall pylon, from where a footpath crosses the fields to pass beneath a railway viaduct and the canal aqueduct, before climbing up to the towpath, and turning left.

The Way leaves the canal briefly to bypass a narrow tunnel, climbing up to pass Hydebank Farm before bearing left down the hill to rejoin the towpath. This is very soon left once more, however, to follow a splendid woodland terrace path through Kirk Wood. This descends by a stepped path to the Chadkirk Country Estate. The Way follows the estate road from here down to the main road (A627), where it turns left.

The road is left once more on the next bend, where a farm road takes over, leading straight ahead. At the entrance to a farm (kennels) the route turns right with the track, continuing past a second farm and staying with the track. After leaving the woods, a waymarked path on the left leads down to cross the river Goyt. The path climbs up the rise left, bearing right then to follow a course parallel to the river.

The river is followed more or less faithfully all the way through to Stockport's Vernon Park, bearing right to pass first a cricket field and later a sports ground, before emerging into the park, where the route keeps to the right along the clifftop. Turning right before the museum building (by a large urn) the path is followed to the road (B6104), where the Way turns right.

After crossing the river Goyt for the last time, the Way turns left into Welkin Road, which is followed to the end, by the mill at the foot of the motorway embankment. It turns left here, then right under the motorway, continuing ahead to join the course of a disused railway. After passing through the Brinnington Tunnel, the Way continues along the track, to merge with the Trans Pennine Trail.

With your arrival at the A626 road, your epic journey is over. But, unless things have improved since the writer was here, do not expect a 21 gun salute or a fanfare of trumpets. You will be lucky if you can find any tangible confirmation that this is the terminal point of the Midshires Way. Perhaps 'they' are still working out the form it should take!

The Midshires Way
Information and accommodation

LEICESTERSHIRE

Tourist Information Centres
Leicester – Town Hall Square. Tel: 0116 2511301.
Market Harborough – Pen Lloyd Library. Tel: 01858 468106.
Melton Mowbray – Melton Carnegie Museum. Tel: 01664 480992.
Loughborough – John Storer House, Wards End. Tel: 01509 218113.

Accommodation
Hallaton – The Bewicke Arms. Tel: 01858 552517.
Glooston – The Old Barn Inn & Restaurant. Tel: 01858 545215.
Tugby – Mrs Brooks, Whiteacres, Main Street. Tel: 0116 2598365.
Cold Newton – Mrs Johnson, Quenby Lodge. Tel: 0116 2595206.
Gaddesby – The Cheney Arms. Tel: 01664 840260.
Grimston – Mrs Johnston, Church Farm. Tel: 01664 812506.
Old Dalby – Mrs Anderson, Home Farm. Tel: 01664 822622.

Busline
Leicester – Tel: 0116 2511411.

NOTTINGHAMSHIRE

Tourist Information Centre
Nottingham – 1 Smithy Row. Tel: 0115 9470661.

Busline
Nottingham – Tel: 0115 9240000.

DERBYSHIRE

Tourist Information Centres
Derby – Market Place. Tel: 01332 255802.
Matlock Bath – The Pavilion. Tel: 01629 55082.
Buxton – The Crescent. Tel: 01298 25106.
New Mills – Heritage Centre. Tel: 01663 746904.

Accommodation

Ambergate – Shining Cliff YHA. Tel: 01629 825850.
Alderwasley – Ye Old Bear (inc. caravan). Tel: 01629 822585.
Middleton by Wirksworth – The Rising Sun. Tel: 01629 822420.
Brassington – The Miners Arms. Tel: 01629 540222.
Hartington – YHA. Tel: 01298 84223.
Hurdlow – The Bull i' th' Thorn (inc. camping, caravan site, holiday flat).
   Tel: 01298 83348.
Chelmorton – The Church Inn. Tel: 01298 85319.
Buxton – YHA. Tel: 01298 22287.
Furness Vale – The Soldier Dick. Tel: 01663 743868.

Busline

Derby – Tel: 01332 292200.
Buxton – Tel: 01298 23098.

STOCKPORT METROPOLITAN BOROUGH

Tourist Information Centre

Stockport – 9 Princes Street. Tel: 0161 4743320.

Busline

Greater Manchester – Tel: 0161 2287811.
Cheshire – Tel: 01244 602666 or 01625 534850.